Hopes and Impediments

Books by Chinua Achebe

THE SACRIFICIAL EGG AND OTHER STORIES
THINGS FALL APART
NO LONGER AT EASE
CHIKE AND THE RIVER
A MAN OF THE PEOPLE
ARROW OF GOD
GIRLS AT WAR AND OTHER STORIES
BEWARE SOUL BROTHER
MORNING YET ON CREATION DAY
THE TROUBLE WITH NIGERIA
THE FLUTE
THE DRUM
ANTHILLS OF THE SAVANNAH
HOPES AND IMPEDIMENTS: SELECTED ESSAYS
HOW THE LEOPARD GOT HIS CLAWS (with John
    Iroaganachi)
WINDS OF CHANGE: MODERN SHORT STORIES
    FROM BLACK AFRICA (with Others)
AFRICAN SHORT STORIES (with C. L. Innes, Eds.)

CHINUA ACHEBE

HOPES

 AND

IMPEDIMENTS

 Selected Essays

DOUBLEDAY

New York · London · Toronto · Sydney · Auckland

Published by Doubleday, a division of
Bantam Doubleday Dell Publishing Group, Inc.
666 Fifth Avenue, New York, New York 10103

DOUBLEDAY and the portrayal of an anchor with a dolphin are
trademarks of Doubleday, a division of
Bantam Doubleday Dell Publishing Group, Inc.

Library of Congress Cataloging-in-Publication Data
Achebe, Chinua.
    Hopes and impediments : selected essays / Chinua Achebe. — 1st
American ed.
        p.   cm.
    Bibliography: p.
    Includes index.
    ISBN 0-385-24730-3
    I. Title.
PR9387.9.A3H6   1989
809—dc19   89-31281
                                                                      CIP

ISBN 0-385-24730-3
Originally published in Great Britain by Heinemann
Copyright © 1988 by Chinua Achebe
All Rights Reserved
Printed in the United States of America
October 1989
First American Edition

Contents

Contents

Acknowledgments

The author and publisher would like to thank the following for permission to use material in this book.

University of Massachusetts, Amherst, The Chancellor's Lecture Series, 1974–75, Amherst 1976, and *Massachusetts Review*, vol. 18, no. 4, winter 1977, Amherst, for "An Image of Africa: Racism in Conrad's *Heart of Darkness.*"

The Times Literary Supplement, 1 February 1980, for "Impediments to Dialogue Between North and South."

New Letters, vol. 40, Kansas City, October 1973, for "Named for Victoria, Queen of England."

New Statesman, London, 29 January 1965, for "The Novelist as Teacher."

University of California at Los Angeles, Regents' Lecture, 1984 for "The Writer and His Community."

Herbert M. Cole and Chike C. Aniakor, authors, and Museum of Cultural History, University of California at Los Angeles, publishers of *Igbo Arts: Community and Cosmos*, 1984, for "The Igbo World and Its Art."

Dalhousie Review, vol. 53, no. 4, Halifax, Canada, December 1973, for "Thoughts on the African Novel."

University of Ibadan, The Equiano Memorial Lecture, 1977, and *Okike*, no. 14, September 1978, Nsukka, for "Work and Play in Tutuola's *The Palm-Wine Drinkard.*"

Fourth Dimension Publishers, publishers of *Don't Let Him Die*, Enugu, 1978, for "Don't Let Him Die: A Tribute to Christopher Okigbo."

Kofi Awoonor, author, and Doubleday/Anchor, New York, publishers of *This Earth, My Brother* . . . , 1971, for "Kofi Awoonor as a Novelist."

Dartmouth College, New Hampshire, U.S.A., for "Language and the Destiny of Man."

University of Ife, Convocation Lecture, 1978, for "The Truth of Fiction."

Author's Preface

THIS SELECTION from essays I wrote for diverse occasions over a period of twenty-three years represents my abiding concerns in literature and the arts as well as my interest in wider social issues. In bringing the work together into one volume, I might simply have arranged the items in chronological order. Instead, and following a certain whim, I took my standard-bearer from the middle ranks and then picked my way back and forth to position the rest. James Baldwin's death in November 1987, while the manuscript was in active production with my publishers, determined the final stop-press entry.

But stepping back and looking at this somewhat haphazard organization I now perceive a certain unpremeditated roundedness to the final result. To open the collection with a 1974 public lecture on Conrad's racism given at the University of Massachusetts, Amherst, and also close it at the same institution thirteen years later with a tribute to one of the most intrepid fighters against racism, was, at the very least, a curious coincidence.

Conrad and Baldwin; two very different writers separated by almost every barrier we cherish—*time* (Baldwin was born the very year Conrad died); *space* (a Polish exile in England and an American exile in France); and, greatest of all perhaps, *race* (one white and the other black).

This last turns out to be the most crucial in its consequences, for while Conrad casually wrote words that continue to give morale to the barricades of racism, Baldwin spent his talents subverting them. Impediments and Hopes!

At the reception that followed my 1974 lecture an elderly English professor had walked up to me and said: "How dare you!" and stalked away. A few days later another English professor said to me: "After hearing you the other night I now realize that I had never really read *Heart of Darkness* although I have taught it for years," or words to that effect. Revisiting Amherst thirteen years later in 1987, yet another colleague tells me he did not agree with me before but now does! More hopes?

I am not so naïve as to think that I have slain the monster of racist habit with one stroke of the essay. The twentieth century was ushered in with a prophecy by one of its greatest thinkers, W. E. B. Du Bois (another exile, by the way, who at the very end of a long life of struggle against the monster finally gave America up as a bad job and settled for Nkrumah's Ghana). In the preface of his famous book, *The Souls of Black Folk*, he wrote: "The problem of the Twentieth Century is the problem of the colour line" (New American Library Edition, New York, 1969, p. xi). The verb he used is interesting: *is* instead of *will be*. And he wrote his words not during the 1960s Civil Rights marches in America as the tone might suggest to some, but actually in 1903—"at the dawning of the Twentieth Century" as he himself put it, and only one year later than Conrad's *Heart of Darkness*. This chronology is of the utmost importance. Therefore the defence sometimes proffered: that Conrad should not be judged by the standards of later times; that racism had not become an issue in the world when he wrote his famous African novel, will have to clarify whose world it is talking about.

CHINUA ACHEBE
University of Massachusetts
Amherst

Hopes and Impediments

1

 An Image of Africa:
Racism in Conrad's
Heart of Darkness

I N THE FALL of 1974 I was walking one day from the English Department at the University of Massachusetts to a parking lot. It was a fine autumn morning such as encouraged friendliness to passing strangers. Brisk youngsters were hurrying in all directions, many of them obviously freshmen in their first flush of enthusiasm. An older man going the same way as I turned and remarked to me how very young they came these days. I agreed. Then he asked me if I was a student too. I said no, I was a teacher. What did I teach? African literature. Now that was funny, he said, because he

This is an amended version of the second Chancellor's Lecture at the University of Massachusetts, Amherst, February 1975; later published in the *Massachusetts Review*, vol. 18, no. 4, winter 1977, Amherst.

knew a fellow who taught the same thing, or perhaps it was African *history,* in a certain community college not far from here. It always surprised him, he went on to say, because he never had thought of Africa as having that kind of stuff, you know. By this time I was walking much faster. "Oh well," I heard him say finally, behind me: "I guess I have to take your course to find out."

A few weeks later I received two very touching letters from high school children in Yonkers, New York, who— bless their teacher—had just read *Things Fall Apart.* One of them was particularly happy to learn about the customs and superstitions of an African tribe.

I propose to draw from these rather trivial encounters rather heavy conclusions which at first sight might seem somewhat out of proportion to them. But only, I hope, at first sight.

The young fellow from Yonkers, perhaps partly on account of his age, but I believe also for much deeper and more serious reasons, is obviously unaware that the life of his own tribesmen in Yonkers, New York, is full of odd customs and superstitions and, like everybody else in his culture, imagines that he needs a trip to Africa to encounter those things.

The other person being fully my own age could not be excused on the grounds of his years. Ignorance might be a more likely reason; but here again I believe that something more wilful than a mere lack of information was at work. For did not that erudite British historian and Regius Professor at Oxford, Hugh Trevor-Roper, also pronounce that African history did not exist?

If there is something in these utterances more than youthful inexperience, more than a lack of factual knowledge, what is it? Quite simply it is the desire—one might indeed say the need—in Western psychology to set Africa up as a foil to Europe, as a place of negations at once remote and vaguely familiar, in comparison with which Europe's own state of spiritual grace will be manifest.

This need is not new; which should relieve us all of considerable responsibility and perhaps make us even willing to look at this phenomenon dispassionately. I have neither the wish nor the competence to embark on the exercise with the tools of the social and biological sciences but do so more simply in the manner of a novelist responding to one famous book of European fiction: Joseph Conrad's *Heart of Darkness,* which better than any other work that I know displays that Western desire and need which I have just referred to. Of course there are whole libraries of books devoted to the same purpose but most of them are so obvious and so crude that few people worry about them today. Conrad, on the other hand, is undoubtedly one of the great stylists of modern fiction and a good story-teller into the bargain. His contribution therefore falls automatically into a different class— permanent literature—read and taught and constantly evaluated by serious academics. *Heart of Darkness* is indeed so secure today that a leading Conrad scholar has numbered it "among the half-dozen greatest short novels in the English language."[1] I will return to this critical opinion in due course because it may seriously modify my earlier suppositions about who may or may not be guilty in some of the matters I will now raise.

Heart of Darkness projects the image of Africa as "the other world," the antithesis of Europe and therefore of civilization, a place where man's vaunted intelligence and refinement are finally mocked by triumphant bestiality. The book opens on the River Thames, tranquil, resting peacefully "at the decline of day after ages of good service done to the race that peopled its banks."[2] But the actual story will take place on the River Congo, the very antithesis of the Thames. The River Congo is quite decidedly not a River Emeritus. It has rendered no service and enjoys no old-age pension. We are told that "going up that river was like travelling back to the earliest beginning of the world."

Is Conrad saying then that these two rivers are very different, one good, the other bad? Yes, but that is not the real point. It is not the differentness that worries Conrad but the lurking hint of kinship, of common ancestry. For the Thames too "has been one of the dark places of the earth." It conquered its darkness, of course, and is now in daylight and at peace. But if it were to visit its primordial relative, the Congo, it would run the terrible risk of hearing grotesque echoes of its own forgotten darkness, and falling victim to an avenging recrudescence of the mindless frenzy of the first beginnings.

These suggestive echoes comprise Conrad's famed evocation of the African atmosphere in *Heart of Darkness.* In the final consideration, his method amounts to no more than a steady, ponderous, fake-ritualistic repetition of two antithetical sentences, one about silence and the other about frenzy. We can inspect samples of this on pages 103 and 105 of the New American Library edition: (a) "It was the stillness of an implacable force brooding over an inscrutable intention" and (b) "The steamer toiled along slowly on the edge of a black and incomprehensible frenzy." Of course, there is a judicious change of adjective from time to time, so that instead of "inscrutable," for example, you might have "unspeakable," even plain "mysterious," etc., etc.

The eagle-eyed English critic F. R. Leavis[3] drew attention long ago to Conrad's "adjectival insistence upon inexpressible and incomprehensible mystery." That insistence must not be dismissed lightly, as many Conrad critics have tended to do, as a mere stylistic flaw; for it raises serious questions of artistic good faith. When a writer while pretending to record scenes, incidents, and their impact is in reality engaged in inducing hypnotic stupor in his readers through a bombardment of emotive words and other forms of trickery, much more has to be at stake than stylistic felicity. Generally, normal readers are well armed to detect and resist such underhand activity. But Conrad chose his subject well—one which was guaranteed not to put him in conflict with the psychological predisposition of his readers or raise the need for him to contend with their resistance. He chose the role of purveyor of comforting myths.

The most interesting and revealing passages in *Heart of Darkness* are, however, about people. I must crave the indulgence of my reader to quote almost a whole page from about the middle of the story when representatives of Europe in a steamer going down the Congo encounter the denizens of Africa:

> We were wanderers on a prehistoric earth, on an earth that wore the aspect of an unknown planet. We could have fancied ourselves the first of men taking possession of an accursed inheritance, to be subdued at the cost of profound anguish and of excessive toil. But suddenly, as we struggled round a bend, there would be a glimpse of rush walls, of peaked grass-roofs, a burst of yells, a whirl of black limbs, a mass of hands clapping, of feet stamping, of bodies swaying, of eyes rolling, under the droop of heavy and motionless foliage. The steamer toiled along slowly on the edge of the black and incomprehensible frenzy. The prehistoric man was cursing us, praying to us, welcoming us— who could tell? We were cut off from the comprehension of our sur-

roundings; we glided past like phantoms, wondering and secretly ap-
palled, as sane men would be before an enthusiastic outbreak in a
madhouse. We could not understand because we were too far and
could not remember because we were travelling in the night of first
ages, of those ages that are gone, leaving hardly a sign—and no memories.

The earth seemed unearthly. We are accustomed to look upon the
shackled form of a conquered monster, but there—there you could
look at a thing monstrous and free. It was unearthly, and the men
were—No, they were not inhuman. Well, you know, that was the
worst of it—this suspicion of their not being inhuman. It would come
slowly to one. They howled and leaped, and spun, and made horrid
faces; but what thrilled you was just the thought of their humanity—
like yours—the thought of your remote kinship with this wild and
passionate uproar. Ugly. Yes, it was ugly enough; but if you were man
enough you would admit to yourself that there was in you just the
faintest trace of a response to the terrible frankness of that noise, a dim
suspicion of there being a meaning in it which you—you so remote
from the night of first ages—could comprehend.[4]

Herein lies the meaning of *Heart of Darkness* and the
fascination it holds over the Western mind: "What thrilled
you was just the thought of their humanity—like yours . . .
Ugly."

Having shown us Africa in the mass, Conrad then zeros
in, half a page later, on a specific example, giving us one of
his rare descriptions of an African who is not just limbs or
rolling eyes:

And between whiles I had to look after the savage who was fireman.
He was an improved specimen; he could fire up a vertical boiler. He
was there below me, and, upon my word, to look at him was as
edifying as seeing a dog in a parody of breeches and a feather hat,
walking on his hind legs. A few months of training had done for that

really fine chap. He squinted at the steam gauge and at the water gauge with an evident effort of intrepidity—and he had filed his teeth, too, the poor devil, and the wool of his pate shaved into queer patterns, and three ornamental scars on each of his cheeks. He ought to have been clapping his hands and stamping his feet on the bank, instead of which he was hard at work, a thrall to strange witchcraft, full of improving knowledge.[5]

As everybody knows, Conrad is a romantic on the side. He might not exactly admire savages clapping their hands and stamping their feet but they have at least the merit of being in their place, unlike this dog in a parody of breeches. For Conrad, things being in their place is of the utmost importance.

"Fine fellows—cannibals—in their place," he tells us pointedly. Tragedy begins when things leave their accustomed place, like Europe leaving its safe stronghold between the policeman and the baker to take a peep into the heart of darkness.

Before the story takes us into the Congo basin proper we are given this nice little vignette as an example of things in their place:

Now and then a boat from the shore gave one a momentary contact with reality. It was paddled by black fellows. You could see from afar the white of their eyeballs glistening. They shouted, sang; their bodies streamed with perspiration; they had faces like grotesque masks—these chaps; but they had bone, muscle, a wild vitality, an intense energy of movement, that was as natural and true as the surf along their coast. They wanted no excuse for being there. They were a great comfort to look at.[6]

Towards the end of the story Conrad lavishes a whole page quite unexpectedly on an African woman who has obviously been some kind of mistress to Mr. Kurtz and now presides (if I may be permitted a little liberty) like a formidable mystery over the inexorable imminence of his departure:

> She was savage and superb, wild-eyed and magnificent. . . . She stood looking at us without a stir and like the wilderness itself, with an air of brooding over an inscrutable purpose.

This Amazon is drawn in considerable detail, albeit of a predictable nature, for two reasons. First, she is in her place and so can win Conrad's special brand of approval; and second, she fulfils a structural requirement of the story; a savage counterpart to the refined, European woman who will step forth to end the story:

> She came forward, all in black with a pale head, floating toward me in the dusk. She was in mourning . . . She took both my hands in hers and murmured, "I had heard you were coming" . . . She had a mature capacity for fidelity, for belief, for suffering.[7]

The difference in the attitude of the novelist to these two women is conveyed in too many direct and subtle ways to need elaboration. But perhaps the most significant difference is the one implied in the author's bestowal of human expression to the one and the withholding of it from the other. It is clearly not part of Conrad's purpose to confer language on the "rudimentary souls" of Africa. In place of speech they made "a violent babble of uncouth sounds." They "exchanged short grunting phrases" even among themselves. But most of the time they were too busy with their frenzy. There are two occasions in the book, however, when Conrad departs somewhat from his practice and confers speech, even English speech, on the savages. The first occurs when cannibalism gets the better of them:

"Catch 'im," he snapped, with a bloodshot widening of his eyes and a flash of sharp white teeth—"catch 'im. Give 'im to us." "To you, eh?" I asked; "what would you do with them?" "Eat 'im!" he said curtly.[8]

The other occasion was the famous announcement: "Mistah Kurtz—he dead."[9]

At first sight these instances might be mistaken for unexpected acts of generosity from Conrad. In reality they constitute some of his best assaults. In the case of the cannibals the incomprehensible grunts that had thus far served them for speech suddenly proved inadequate for Conrad's purpose of letting the European glimpse the unspeakable craving in their hearts. Weighing the necessity for consistency in the portrayal of the dumb brutes against the sensational advantages of securing their conviction by clear, unambiguous evidence issuing out of their own mouths, Conrad chose the latter. As for the announcement of Mr. Kurtz's death by the "insolent black head in the doorway," what better or more appropriate *finis* could be written to the horror story of that wayward child of civilization who wilfully had given his soul to the powers of darkness and "taken a high seat amongst the devils of the land" than the proclamation of his physical death by the forces he had joined?

It might be contended, of course, that the attitude to the African in *Heart of Darkness* is not Conrad's but that of his fictional narrator, Marlow, and that far from endorsing it Conrad might indeed be holding it up to irony and criticism. Certainly, Conrad appears to go to considerable pains to set up layers of insulation between himself and the moral universe of his story. He has, for example, a narrator behind a narrator. The primary narrator is Marlow, but his account is given to us through the filter of a second, shadowy person.

But if Conrad's intention is to draw a cordon sanitaire between himself and the moral and psychological *malaise* of his narrator, his care seems to me totally wasted because he neglects to hint, clearly and adequately, at an alternative frame of reference by which we may judge the actions and opinions of his characters. It would not have been beyond Conrad's power to make that provision if he had thought it necessary. Conrad seems to me to approve of Marlow, with only minor reservations—a fact reinforced by the similarities between their two careers.

Marlow comes through to us not only as a witness of truth, but one holding those advanced and humane views appropriate to the English liberal tradition which required all Englishmen of decency to be deeply shocked by atrocities in Bulgaria or the Congo of King Leopold of the Belgians or wherever.

Thus, Marlow is able to toss out such bleeding-heart sentiments as these:

> They were all dying slowly—it was very clear. They were not enemies, they were not criminals, they were nothing earthly now—nothing but black shadows of disease and starvation, lying confusedly in the greenish gloom. Brought from all the recesses of the coast in all the legality of time contracts, lost in uncongenial surroundings, fed on unfamiliar food, they sickened, became inefficient, and were then allowed to crawl away and rest.[10]

The kind of liberalism espoused here by Marlow/Conrad touched all the best minds of the age in England, Europe and America. It took different forms in the minds of different people but almost always managed to sidestep the ultimate question of equality between white people and black people. That extraordinary missionary Albert Schweitzer, who sacrificed brilliant careers in music and theology in Europe for a life of service to Africans in much the same area as Conrad writes about, epitomizes the ambivalence. In a comment which has often been quoted Schweitzer says: "The African is indeed my brother but my junior brother." And so he proceeded to build a hospital appropriate to the needs of junior brothers with standards of hygiene reminiscent of medical practice in the days before the germ theory of disease came into being. Naturally he became a sensation in Europe and America. Pilgrims flocked, and I believe still flock even after he has passed on, to witness the prodigious miracle in Lambaréné, on the edge of the primeval forest.

Conrad's liberalism would not take him quite as far as Schweitzer's, though. He would not use the word "brother" however qualified; the farthest he would go was "kinship." When Marlow's African helmsman falls down with a spear in his heart he gives his white master one final disquieting look:

> And the intimate profundity of that look he gave me when he received his hurt remains to this day in my memory—like a claim of distant kinship affirmed in a supreme moment.[11]

It is important to note that Conrad, careful as ever with his words, is concerned not so much about "distant kinship" as about someone *laying a claim* on it. The black man lays a claim on the white man which is well-nigh intolerable. It is the laying of this claim which frightens and at the same time fascinates Conrad, "the thought of their humanity—like yours . . . Ugly."

The point of my observations should be quite clear by now, namely that Joseph Conrad was a thoroughgoing racist. That this simple truth is glossed over in criticisms of his work is due to the fact that white racism against Africa is such a normal way of thinking that its manifestations go completely unremarked. Students of *Heart of Darkness* will often tell you that Conrad is concerned not so much with Africa as with the deterioration of one European mind caused by solitude and sickness. They will point out to you that Conrad is, if anything, less charitable to the Europeans in the story than he is to the natives, that the point of the story is to ridicule Europe's civilizing mission in Africa. A Conrad student informed me in Scotland that Africa is merely a setting for the disintegration of the mind of Mr. Kurtz.

Which is partly the point. Africa as setting and backdrop which eliminates the African as human factor. Africa as a metaphysical battlefield devoid of all recognizable humanity, into which the wandering European enters at his peril. Can nobody see the preposterous and perverse arrogance in thus reducing Africa to the role of props for the break-up of one petty European mind? But that is not even the point. The real question is the dehumanization of Africa and Africans which this age-long attitude has fostered and continues to foster in the world. And the question is whether a novel which celebrates this dehumanization, which depersonalizes a portion of the human race, can be called a great work of art. My answer is: No, it cannot. I do not doubt Conrad's great talents. Even *Heart of Darkness* has its memorably good passages and moments:

> The reaches opened before us and closed behind, as if the forest had stepped leisurely across the water to bar the way for our return.

Its exploration of the minds of the European characters is often penetrating and full of insight. But all that has been more than fully discussed in the last fifty years. His obvious racism has, however, not been addressed. And it is high time it was!

Conrad was born in 1857, the very year in which the first Anglican missionaries were arriving among my own people in Nigeria. It was certainly not his fault that he lived his life at a time when the reputation of the black man was at a particularly low level. But even after due allowances have been made for all the influences of contemporary prejudice on his sensibility, there remains still in Conrad's attitude a residue of antipathy to black people which his peculiar psychology alone can explain. His own account of his first encounter with a black man is very revealing:

> A certain enormous buck nigger encountered in Haiti fixed my conception of blind, furious, unreasoning rage, as manifested in the human animal to the end of my days. Of the nigger I used to dream for years afterwards.[12]

Certainly Conrad had a problem with niggers. His inordinate love of that word itself should be of interest to psychoanalysts. Sometimes his fixation on blackness is equally interesting, as when he gives us this brief description: "A black figure stood up, strode on long black legs, waving long black arms"[13]—as though we might expect a black figure striding along on black legs to wave white arms! But so unrelenting is Conrad's obsession.

As a matter of interest, Conrad gives us in *A Personal Record* what amounts to a companion piece to the buck nigger of Haiti. At the age of sixteen Conrad encountered his first Englishman in Europe. He calls him "my unforgettable Englishman" and describes him in the following manner:

[his] calves exposed to the public gaze . . . dazzled the beholder by
the splendour of their marble-like condition and their rich tone of
young ivory . . . The light of a headlong, exalted satisfaction with
the world of men . . . illumined his face . . . and triumphant eyes.
In passing he cast a glance of kindly curiosity and a friendly gleam of
big, sound, shiny teeth . . . his white calves twinkled sturdily.[14]

Irrational love and irrational hate jostling together in the
heart of that talented, tormented man. But whereas irrational
love may at worst engender foolish acts of indiscretion, irrational hate can endanger the life of the community. Naturally, Conrad is a dream for psychoanalytic critics. Perhaps
the most detailed study of him in this direction is by Bernard
C. Meyer, M.D. In his lengthy book, Dr. Meyer follows every
conceivable lead (and sometime inconceivable ones) to explain Conrad. As an example, he gives us long disquisitions
on the significance of hair and hair-cutting in Conrad. And
yet not even one word is spared for his attitude to black
people. Not even the discussion of Conrad's antisemitism was
enough to spark off in Dr. Meyer's mind those other dark
and explosive thoughts. Which only leads one to surmise that
Western psychoanalysts must regard the kind of racism displayed by Conrad as absolutely normal despite the profoundly important work done by Frantz Fanon in the psychi-
atric hospitals of French Algeria.

Whatever Conrad's problems were, you might say he is
now safely dead. Quite true. Unfortunately, his heart of darkness plagues us still. Which is why an offensive and deplor-
able book can be described by a serious scholar as "among
the half-dozen greatest short novels in the English language." And why it is today perhaps the most commonly

prescribed novel in twentieth-century literature courses in English departments of American universities.

There are two probable grounds on which what I have said so far may be contested. The first is that it is no concern of fiction to please people about whom it is written. I will go along with that. But I am not talking about pleasing people. I am talking about a book which parades in the most vulgar fashion prejudices and insults from which a section of mankind has suffered untold agonies and atrocities in the past and continues to do so in many ways and many places today. I am talking about a story in which the very humanity of black people is called in question.

Secondly, I may be challenged on the grounds of actuality. Conrad, after all, did sail down the Congo in 1890 when my own father was still a babe in arms. How could I stand up more than fifty years after his death and purport to contradict him? My answer is that as a sensible man I will not accept just any traveller's tales solely on the grounds that I have not made the journey myself. I will not trust the evidence even of a man's very eyes when I suspect them to be as jaundiced as Conrad's. And we also happen to know that Conrad was, in the words of his biographer, Bernard C. Meyer, "notoriously inaccurate in the rendering of his own history."[15]

But more important by far is the abundant testimony about Conrad's savages which we could gather if we were so inclined from other sources and which might lead us to think that these people must have had other occupations besides merging into the evil forest or materializing out of it simply to plague Marlow and his dispirited band. For as it happened, soon after Conrad had written his book an event of far greater consequence was taking place in the art world of

Europe. This is how Frank Willett, a British art historian, describes it:

> Gauguin had gone to Tahiti, the most extravagant individual act of turning to a non-European culture in the decades immediately before and after 1900, when European artists were avid for new artistic experiences, but it was only about 1904–5 that African art began to make its distinctive impact. One piece is still identifiable; it is a mask that had been given to Maurice Vlaminck in 1905. He records that Derain was "speechless" and "stunned" when he saw it, bought it from Vlaminck and in turn showed it to Picasso and Matisse, who were also greatly affected by it. Ambroise Vollard then borrowed it and had it cast in bronze . . . The revolution of twentieth century art was under way![16]

The mask in question was made by other savages living just north of Conrad's River Congo. They have a name too: the Fang people, and are without a doubt among the world's greatest masters of the sculptured form. The event Frank Willett is referring to marked the beginning of cubism and the infusion of new life into European art that had run completely out of strength.

The point of all this is to suggest that Conrad's picture of the peoples of the Congo seems grossly inadequate even at the height of their subjection to the ravages of King Leopold's International Association for the Civilization of Central Africa.

Travellers with closed minds can tell us little except about themselves. But even those not blinkered, like Conrad, with xenophobia, can be astonishingly blind. Let me digress a little here. One of the greatest and most intrepid travellers of all time, Marco Polo, journeyed to the Far East from the Mediterranean in the thirteenth century and spent twenty years in the court of Kublai Khan in China. On his return to Venice he set down in his book entitled *Description of the World* his impressions of the peoples and places and customs he had seen. But there were at least two extraordinary omissions in his account. He said nothing about the art of printing, unknown as yet in Europe but in full flower in China. He either did not notice it at all or, if he did, failed to see what use Europe could possibly have for it. Whatever the reason, Europe had to wait another hundred years for Gutenberg. But even more spectacular was Marco Polo's omission of any reference to the Great Wall of China, nearly four thousand miles long and already more than one thousand years old at the time of his visit. Again, he may not have seen it; but the Great Wall of China is the only structure built by man which is visible from the moon![17] Indeed, travellers can be blind.

As I said earlier Conrad did not originate the image of Africa which we find in his book. It was and is the dominant image of Africa in the Western imagination and Conrad merely brought the peculiar gifts of his own mind to bear on it. For reasons which can certainly use close psychological inquiry, the West seems to suffer deep anxieties about the precariousness of its civilization and to have a need for constant reassurance by comparison with Africa. If Europe, advancing in civilization, could cast a backward glance periodically at Africa trapped in primordial barbarity it could say with faith and feeling: There go I but for the grace of God. Africa is to Europe as the picture is to Dorian Gray—a carrier on to whom the master unloads his physical and moral deformities so that he may go forward, erect and immaculate. Consequently, Africa is something to be avoided just as the picture has to be hidden away to safeguard the man's jeopardous integrity. Keep away from Africa, or else! Mr. Kurtz of *Heart of Darkness* should have heeded that warning and the prowling horror in his heart would have kept its place, chained to its lair. But he foolishly exposed himself to the wild irresistible allure of the jungle and lo! the darkness found him out.

In my original conception of this essay I had thought to conclude it nicely on an appropriately positive note in which I would suggest from my privileged position in African and Western cultures some advantages the West might derive from Africa once it rid its mind of old prejudices and began to look at Africa not through a haze of distortions and cheap mystifications but quite simply as a continent of people—not angels, but not rudimentary souls either—just people, often highly gifted people and often strikingly successful in their enterprise with life and society. But as I thought more about the stereotype image, about its grip and pervasiveness, about the wilful tenacity with which the West holds it to its heart; when I thought of the West's television and cinema and newspapers, about books read in its schools and out of school, of churches preaching to empty pews about the need to send help to the heathen in Africa, I realized that no easy optimism was possible. And there was in any case something totally wrong in offering bribes to the West in return for its good opinion of Africa. Ultimately the abandonment of unwholesome thoughts must be its own and only reward. Although I have used the word "wilful" a few times here to characterize the West's view of Africa, it may well be that what is happening at this stage is more akin to reflex action than calculated malice. Which does not make the situation more but less hopeful.

The *Christian Science Monitor,* a paper more enlightened

than most, once carried an interesting article written by its Education Editor on the serious psychological and learning problems faced by little children who speak one language at home and then go to school where something else is spoken. It was a wide-ranging article taking in Spanish-speaking children in America, the children of migrant Italian workers in Germany, the quadrilingual phenomenon in Malaysia and so on. And all this while the article speaks unequivocally about language. But then out of the blue sky comes this:

> In London there is an enormous immigration of children who speak Indian or Nigerian dialects, or some other native language.[18]

I believe that the introduction of "dialects," which is technically erroneous in the context, is almost a reflex action caused by an instinctive desire of the writer to downgrade the discussion to the level of Africa and India. And this is quite comparable to Conrad's withholding of language from his rudimentary souls. Language is too grand for these chaps; let's give them dialects!

In all this business a lot of violence is inevitably done not only to the image of despised peoples but even to words, the very tools of possible redress. Look at the phrase "native language" in the *Christian Science Monitor* excerpt. Surely the only *native* language possible in London is Cockney English. But our writer means something else—something appropriate to the sounds Indians and Africans make!

Although the work of redressing which needs to be done may appear too daunting, I believe it is not one day too soon to begin. Conrad saw and condemned the evil of imperial exploitation but was strangely unaware of the racism on which it sharpened its iron tooth. But the victims of racist slander who for centuries have had to live with the inhumanity it makes them heir to have always known better than any casual visitor, even when he comes loaded with the gifts of a Conrad.

2

 Impediments
to Dialogue
 Between North
and South

IN 1979 I WAS ASKED in a long cable if I would agree
to make an opening statement at a festival of African arts in
Berlin. A topic was also proposed to me: The Necessity for
Cultural Exchange in a Spirit of Partnership Between North
and South.

As a rule, I do not agree to speak to prescription. But in
this case the prescription was given with great tact and elegance. And what was more, it coincided almost completely
with my own inclinations. Nevertheless—if only to uphold
my commitment to freedom of choice—I decided to make a
change in the letter of the prescription if not in its spirit.

This is a slightly amended version of the address, which was subsequently
published in *The Times Literary Supplement,* February 1, 1980.

Therefore, rather than talking about the necessity for cultural exchange which, in any case, was self-evident to me, I decided to speak about *the factors that impede* cultural dialogue between North and South, in this case Europe and Africa.

Perhaps I should not conclude this preamble without mentioning that the telex message from Berlin came to me—I might almost say, came *at* me—from three different sources: the Nigerian Airways, the Federal Radio Corporation of Nigeria and the Nigerian Police! So I had it three times, thanks to the thoroughness of the Berlin organizers. My reply, however, was never received as I was to learn on my arrival in Berlin—a perfect example of one-way traffic and a parable of sorts on the situation I was asked to deal with.

The relationship between Europe and Africa is very old and also very special. The coasts of North Africa and Southern Europe interacted intimately to produce the beginnings of modern European civilization. Later, and much less happily, Europe engaged Africa in the tragic misalliance of the slave trade and colonialism to lay the foundations of modern European and American industrialism and wealth. When the poet Sedar Senghor sings of Africa joined to Europe by the navel, he may perhaps overromanticize the relationship, purging it through the benign mother/baby imagery of the cruel malignity that often characterizes Africa's experience with Europe. But even so, he is essentially right about the closeness.

The necessity of cultural exchange in a spirit of partnership between North and South. The key word in the topic proposed to me is "partnership"; it is also the source of the impediment, because no definition of partnership can evade the notion of equality. And equality is the one thing which Europeans are conspicuously incapable of extending to others, especially Africans. Of course partnership as a slogan in political rhetoric is a different matter and is frequently bandied about. But anyone who is in any doubt about its meaning in that context need only be reminded that a British governor of Rhodesia in the 1950s defined the partnership between black and white in his territory, apparently without intending any sarcasm, as the partnership between the horse and its rider!

Although the articulation of the colonial ideal in terms of such starkness might startle reasonable white people into indignant unrecognition, my sense of the situation tells me that in more or less polite formulations *that* was, and is, the fundamental attitude of Europe to Africa. Even the enunciation of the metaphor in human/animal terms is neither new nor accidental.

Let there be no mistake about it. In confronting the black man, the white man has a simple choice: either to accept the black man's humanity and the equality that flows from it, or to reject it and see him as a beast of burden. No middle course exists except as an intellectual quibble. For centuries Europe has chosen the beastly alternative which automatically has ruled out the possibility of a dialogue. You may talk to a horse but you don't wait for a reply!

Because of the myths created by the white man to dehumanize the Negro in the course of the last four hundred years—myths which have yielded perhaps psychological, certainly economic, comfort to Europe—the white man has been talking and talking and never listening because he imagines he has been talking to a dumb beast. In the words of Steve Biko during his last trial in the white, Christian and Western outpost of South Africa: "The integration so achieved is a one-way course, with the whites doing all the talking and the blacks listening."

When Wole Soyinka made the now famous attempt to dismiss the negritude movement by pointing out that a tiger does not talk tigritude, Senghor—one of the founders of the movement—made an adequate reply, namely that a tiger does not talk. Perhaps, on account of its breathtaking simplicity, the depth of meaning of that answer was lost on many people. The Negro talks! And talking is a measure of his humanity.

Let me hasten to add that I am fully aware of the simplifications I am indulging in so that my basic points may stand out. I realize, for instance, that all white people cannot be exactly of one mind or equally guilty of the fault of too much transmission and too little reception; I realize that all European peoples did not participate to the same degree in the events of modern African history. But despite local qualifications that could be made here and there, I believe that the major outline of my thesis is correct.

There is one qualification, however, which I must make because it bears on the prospects of resolving the problem of dialogue. I refer to a certain ambivalent curiosity of the white man about Africans which according to one's nature might be either a source of hope or of despair. Personally, I go along with John Milton: when hope and fear arbitrate the event I incline to the hope rather than the fear.

The hope is that if the white man is so curious about the

black man, one day he may actually stop and listen to him. The fear is that the white man has found and used so many evasions in the past to replace or simulate dialogue to his own satisfaction that he may go on doing it indefinitely.

The first evasion is the phenomenon of the expert or the foreign correspondent. The white man sends one of his fellows to visit the land or the mind of black people and bring home all the news. This has included every kind of traveller: priests, soldiers, bandits, traders, journalists, scholars, explorers and novelists. Don't get me wrong. I do not lump all these characters together in order to dismiss them with the same wave of the hand. That would be foolish, ungracious and false. Many Europeans have made enormous contributions towards the understanding of Africa in Europe. Some of them have even helped us to see ourselves anew in the freshness of an itinerant perspective. But what we are talking about here is dialogue which requires two people and cannot be replaced by even the most brilliant monologue.

As it happens, most of the monologue is not brilliant but foolishly sensational and pretentious. I have drawn attention elsewhere to Joseph Conrad's *Heart of Darkness,* which Europe and America regard as a masterpiece of twentieth-century literature. I have no doubt that the reason for the high standing of this novel is simply that it fortifies racial fears and prejudices and is clever enough to protect itself, should the need arise, with the excuse that it is not really about Africa at all. And yet it is set in Africa and teems with Africans whose humanity is admitted in theory but promptly undermined by the mindlessness of its context and the pretty explicit animal imagery surrounding it. In the entire novel, Conrad allows no more than a dozen words in broken English to one and a half Africans: the cannibal who says

"Catch 'im . . . eat 'im," and the half-caste who announces "Mistah Kurtz—he dead."

Europe's reliance on its own experts would not worry us if it did not, at the same time, attempt to exclude African testimony. But it often does.

Perhaps I would be allowed two liberties: first, to include Americans under the general rubric of "European" (which is what we tend to call them in Africa, anyway) and secondly, to give an example with one of my books.

An American reviewer with the amazing name of Christ writing about *Arrow of God* in the *New York Times Book Review* had this to say:

> Perhaps no Nigerian at the present state of his culture and ours can tell us what we need to know about that country, in a way that is available to our understanding . . . in the way W. H. Hudson made South America real to us, or T. E. Lawrence brought Arabia to life.

Please note that if Mr. Christ had said that a South American had made South America real to him or an Arab, Arabia, I would have accepted my failure modestly and in good grace. But Christ's problem seems to be fundamental: only his brothers can explain the world, even the alien world of strangers, to him! So he sent a brother to South America to tell him all about that continent and then another to Arabia. But before he has had time to dispatch a third brother to report on Nigeria, a Nigerian has jumped the gun and is talking!

So much for the dialogue between the white man and his brother concerning the Negro. It is obviously not working. The Negro talks!

The second evasion of dialogue is the phenomenon of the "authentic African." This creature was invented to circumvent the credibility problem of the white man talking to himself. If, the white man seems to say, I must now listen to Negroes, then I had better find those as yet unspoilt by Western knowledge, which unfortunately tends to put inconvenient words in their mouths. The distinguished German scholar of African culture, the late Janheinz Jahn, who has reflected on this problem, has put it very well:

> Only the most highly cultivated person counts as a "real European." A "real African," on the other hand, lives in the bush . . . goes naked . . . and tells fairy stories about the crocodile and the elephant. The more primitive, the more really African. But an African who is enlightened and cosmopolitan . . . who makes political speeches, or writes novels, no longer counts as a real African.[1]

As the pace of change accelerates there won't, alas, be many "authentic Africans" around with that wholesome and unquestioning admiration for white people which was the chief attraction of the bush African. And in any case the nature of the European in Africa is also changing. A businessman who is there for profit which is no longer safe and guaranteed isn't going to consult a witch doctor for his opinion on an investment risk! So the uses of the "real African" have narrowed drastically.

Which should bring us to the end of the road, if the white man were not so ingenious! The *New York Times Book Review* once carried in the same issue a laudatory review of V. S. Naipaul's novel *A Bend in the River* and also a long interview with him interspersed with commentary by the distinguished American writer and critic Elizabeth Hardwick. Says Hardwick:

> Now [Naipaul] has passed beyond India . . . to a universal "Darkness." Talking to him, reading and re-reading his work, one cannot

help but *[sic]* think . . . of Idi Amin, the Ayatollah Khomeini, of the
fate of Bhutto. These figures of an improbable and deranging transition come to mind because Naipaul's work is a creative reflection upon
a devastating lack of historical preparation, upon the anguish of whole
countries and peoples unable to cope.[2]

Elizabeth Hardwick quotes profusely and with apparent
relish and approval from the growing corpus of scornful
work which Naipaul has written on Africa, India and South
America. Particularly interesting were his Congo travels in
1965, from which he reports on "native people camping in
the ruins of civilization" and the "bush creeping back as you
stood there."

Reading Elizabeth Hardwick's interview, an absurd and
rather pathetic picture rises from the printed page: this
knowledgeable American lady lapping up like a wide-eyed
village girl every drop of pretentiousness that falls from the
lips of this literary guru, a new purveyor of the old comforting myths of her race.

Would it, in the circumstances, be too difficult to wonder
what "devastating lack of historical preparation" created
Hitler, Stalin and Botha; what "deranging transition"
formed the fate of Biko, or Patrice Lumumba, for that matter? Apparently, yes; it would be quite impossible.
Hardwick's last question to Naipaul was, predictably: "What
is the future in Africa?" His reply, pat, smart and equally
predictable: "Africa has no future." This modern Conrad,
who is partly native himself, does not beat about the bush!

The new evasion will have its day and pass on leaving
unsolved the problem of dialogue which has plagued Afro-
European relations for centuries, until Europe is ready. Ready
to concede total African humanity. "We are the white man's

rubbish," says an Athol Fugard character, ". . . his rubbish is people." When that changes, dialogue may have a chance to begin. If the heap of rubbish doesn't catch fire meanwhile and set the world ablaze.

3

Named for Victoria, Queen of England

I WAS BORN IN OGIDI in Eastern Nigeria of devout Christian parents. The line between Christian and non-Christian was much more definite in my village forty years ago than it is today. When I was growing up I remember we tended to look down on the others. We were called in our language "the people of the church" or "the association of God." The others we called, with the conceit appropriate to followers of the true religion, the heathen or even "the people of nothing."

Thinking about it today I am not so sure that it isn't they who should have been looking down on us for our apostasy.

First published in *New Letters*, vol. 40, Kansas City, October 1973; subsequently in *Morning Yet on Creation Day*, Doubleday Anchor Books, 1975.

And perhaps they did. But the bounties of the Christian God were not to be taken lightly—education, paid jobs and many other advantages that nobody in his right senses could under-rate. And in fairness we should add that there was more than naked opportunism in the defection of many to the new religion. For in some ways and in certain circumstances it stood firmly on the side of humane behavior. It said, for instance, that twins were not evil and must no longer be abandoned in the forest to die. Think what that would have done for that unhappy woman whose heart torn to shreds at every birth could now hold on precariously to a new hope.

There was still considerable evangelical fervour in my early days. Once a month in place of the afternoon church service we went into the village with the gospel. We would sing all the way to the selected communal meeting place. Then the pastor or catechist or one of the elders having waited for enough heathen people to assemble would address them on the evil futility of their ways. I do not recall that we made even one conversion. On the contrary, I have a distinct memory of the preacher getting into serious trouble with a villager who was apparently notorious for turning up at every occasion with a different awkward question. As you would expect, this was no common villager but a fallen Christian, technically known as a *backslider*. Like Satan, a spell in heaven had armed him with unfair insights.

My father had joined the new faith as a young man and risen rapidly in its ranks to become an evangelist and church teacher. His maternal uncle, who had brought him up (his own parents having died early), was a man of note in the village. He had taken the highest-but-one title that a man of wealth and honour might aspire to, and the feast he gave the town on his initiation became a byword for open-handedness bordering on prodigality. The grateful and approving community called him henceforth Udo Osinyi—Udo who cooks more than the whole people can eat.

From which you might deduce that my ancestors approved of ostentation. And you would be right. But they would probably have argued if the charge was made by their modern counterparts that in their day wealth could only be acquired honestly, by the sweat of a man's brow. They would probably never have given what I believe was the real but carefully concealed reason, namely that given their extreme republican and egalitarian world-view it made good sense for the community to encourage a man acquiring more wealth than his neighbours to squander it and thus convert a threat of material power into harmless honorific distinction, while his accumulated riches flowed back into the commonwealth.

Apparently the first missionaries who came to my village went to Udo Osinyi to pay their respects and seek support for their work. For a short while he allowed them to operate from his compound. He probably thought it was some kind of circus whose strange presence added lustre to his household. But after a few days he sent them packing again. Not, as you might think, on account of the crazy theology they had begun to propound but on the much more serious grounds of musical aesthetics. Said the old man: "Your singing is too sad to come from a man's house. My neighbours might think it was my funeral dirge."

So they parted—without rancour. When my father joined the missionaries the old man does not seem to have raised any serious objections. Perhaps like Ezeulu he thought he needed a representative in their camp. Or perhaps he thought it was a modern diversion which a young man might indulge in without coming to too much harm. He must have had second thoughts when my father began to have ideas about converting him. But it never came to an open rift; apparently not even a quarrel. They remained very close to the end. I don't know it for certain, but I think the old man was the very embodiment of tolerance, insisting only that whatever a man decided to do he should do it with style. I am told he was very pleased when my father, a teacher now, had a wedding to which white missionaries (now no longer figures of fun) came in their fineries, their men and their women, bearing gifts. He must have been impressed too by the wedding feast, which might not have approached his own legendary performance but was by all accounts pretty lavish.

Before my father died, he had told me of a recent dream in which his uncle, long long dead, arrived at our house like a traveller from a distant land come in for a brief stop and rest and was full of admiration for the zinc house my father had built. There was something between those two that I find deep, moving and perplexing. And of those two generations—defectors and loyalists alike—there was something I have not been able to fathom. That was why the middle story in the Okonkwo trilogy as I originally projected it never got written. I had suddenly become aware that in my gallery of ancestral heroes there is an empty place from which an unknown personage seems to have departed.

I was baptized Albert Chinualumogu. I dropped the tribute to Victorian England when I went to the university although you might find some early acquaintances still calling me by it. The earliest of them all—my mother—certainly stuck to it to the bitter end. So if anyone asks you what Her Britannic Majesty Queen Victoria had in common with Chinua Achebe, the answer is: They both lost their Albert! As for the second name, which in the manner of my people is a full-length philosophical statement, I simply cut it in two, making it more businesslike without, I hope, losing the general drift of its meaning.

I have always been fond of stories and intrigued by language—first Igbo, spoken with such eloquence by the old men of the village, and later English, which I began to learn at about the age of eight. I don't know for certain, but I have probably spoken more words in Igbo than English but I have definitely written more words in English than Igbo. Which I think makes me perfectly bilingual. Some people have suggested that I should be better off writing in Igbo. Sometimes they seek to drive the point home by asking me in which language I dream. When I reply that I dream in both languages they seem not to believe it. More recently I have heard an even more potent and metaphysical version of the question: In what language do you have an orgasm? That should settle the matter if I knew.

We lived at the crossroads of cultures. We still do today; but when I was a boy one could see and sense the peculiar quality and atmosphere of it more clearly. I am not talking about all that rubbish we hear of the spiritual void and mental stresses that Africans are supposed to have, or the evil forces and irrational passions prowling through Africa's heart of darkness. We know the racist mystique behind a lot of that stuff and should merely point out that those who prefer to see Africa in those lurid terms have not themselves demonstrated any clear superiority in sanity or more competence in coping with life.

But still the crossroads does have a certain dangerous potency; dangerous because a man might perish there wrestling with multiple-headed spirits, but also he might be lucky and return to his people with the boon of prophetic vision.

On one arm of the cross we sang hymns and read the Bible night and day. On the other my father's brother and his family, blinded by heathenism, offered food to idols. That was how it was supposed to be anyhow. But I knew without knowing why that it was too simple a way to describe what was going on. Those idols and that food had a strange pull on me in spite of my being such a thorough little Christian that often at Sunday services at the height of the grandeur of "Te Deum Laudamus" I would have dreams of a mantle of gold falling on me as the choir of angels drowned our mortal song and the voice of God Himself thundering: This is my beloved son in whom I am well pleased. Yet, despite those delusions of divine destiny I was not past taking my little sister to our neighbour's house when our parents were not looking and partaking of heathen festival meals. I never found their rice and stew to have the flavour of idolatry. I was about ten then. If anyone likes to believe that I was torn by spiritual agonies or stretched on the rack of my ambivalence, he certainly may suit himself. I do not remember any undue distress. What I do remember is a fascination for the ritual and the life on the other arm of the crossroads. And I believe two things were in my favour—that curiosity, and the little distance imposed between me and it by the accident of my birth. The distance becomes not a separation but a bringing together like the necessary backward step which a judicious viewer may take in order to see a canvas steadily and fully.

I was lucky in having a few old books around the house when I was learning to read. As the fifth in a family of six children and with parents so passionate for their children's education, I inherited many discarded primers and readers. I remember *A Midsummer Night's Dream* in an advanced stage of falling apart. I think it must have been a prose adaptation, simplified and illustrated. I don't remember whether I made anything of it. Except the title. I couldn't get over the strange beauty of it. "A Midsummer Night's Dream." It was a magic phrase—an incantation that conjured up scenes and landscapes of an alien, happy and unattainable land.

I remember also my mother's *Ije Onye Kraist* which must have been an Igbo adaptation of *Pilgrim's Progress*. It could not have been the whole book; it was too thin. But it had some frightening pictures. I recall in particular a most vivid impression of the valley of the shadow of death. I thought a lot about death in those days. There was another little book which frightened and fascinated me. It had drawings of different parts of the human body. But I was primarily interested in what my elder sister told me was the human heart. Since there is a slight confusion in Igbo between heart and soul I took it that that strange thing looking almost like my mother's iron cooking pot turned upside down was the very thing that flew out when a man died and perched on the head of the coffin on the way to the cemetery.

I found some use for most of the books in our house but by no means all. There was one arithmetic book I smuggled out and sold for half a penny which I needed to buy the tasty *elele* some temptress of a woman sold in the little market outside the school. I was found out and my mother, who had never had cause till then to doubt my honesty—laziness, yes, but not theft—received a huge shock. Of course she redeemed the book. I was so ashamed when she brought it home that I don't think I ever looked at it again, which was probably why I never had much use for mathematics.

My parents' reverence for books was almost superstitious;

so my action must have seemed like a form of juvenile simony. My father was much worse than my mother. He never destroyed any paper. When he died we had to make a bonfire of all the hoardings of his long life. I am the very opposite of him in this. I can't stand paper around me. Whenever I see a lot of it I am seized by a mild attack of pyromania. When I die my children will not have a bonfire.

The kind of taste I acquired from the chaotic literature in my father's house can well be imagined. For instance, I became very fond of those aspects of ecclesiastical history as could be garnered from *The West African Churchman's Pamphlet*—a little terror of a booklet prescribing interminable Bible readings morning and night. But it was a veritable gold mine for the kind of information I craved in those days. It had the date of consecration for practically every Anglican bishop who ever served in West Africa; and even more intriguing, the dates of their death. Many of them didn't last very long. I remember one pathetic case (I forget his name) who arrived in Lagos straight from his consecration at St. Paul's Cathedral and was dead within days, and his wife a week or two after him. Those were the days when West Africa was truly the white man's grave, when those great lines were written of which I was at that time unaware:

> Bight of Benin! Bight of Benin!
> Where few come out though many go in!

But the most fascinating information I got from *Pamphlet,* as we called it, was this cryptic entry: "Augustine, Bishop of Hippo, died 430." It had that elusive and eternal quality, a tantalizing unfamiliarity which I always found moving.

I did not know that I was going to be a writer because I did not really know of the existence of such creatures until fairly late. The folk stories my mother and elder sister told me had the immemorial quality of the sky and the forests and the rivers. Later, when I got to know that the European stories I read were written by known people, it still didn't help much. It was the same Europeans who made all the other marvellous things like the motor car. We did not come into it at all. We made nothing that wasn't primitive and heathenish.

The nationalist movement in British West Africa after the Second World War brought about a mental revolution which began to reconcile us to ourselves. It suddenly seemed that we too might have a story to tell. "Rule Britannia!" to which we had marched so unselfconsciously on Empire Day now stuck in our throat.

At the university I read some appalling novels about Africa (including Joyce Cary's much praised *Mister Johnson)* and decided that the story we had to tell could not be told for us by anyone else no matter how gifted or well intentioned.

Although I did not set about it consciously in that solemn way, I now know that my first book, *Things Fall Apart,* was an act of atonement with my past, the ritual return and homage of a prodigal son. But things happen very fast in Africa. I had hardly begun to bask in the sunshine of reconciliation when a new cloud appeared, a new estrangement. Political independence had come. The nationalist leader of yesterday (with whom it had not been too difficult to make common cause) had become the not so attractive party boss. And then things really got going. The party boss was chased out by the bright military boys, new idols of the people. But the party boss knows how to wait, knows by heart the counsel Mother Bedbug gave her little ones when the harassed owner of the bed poured hot water on them: "Be patient," said she, "for what is hot will in the end be cold." What is bright can also get tarnished, like the military boys.

One hears that the party boss is already conducting a whispering campaign: "You done see us chop," he says, "now you see *dem* chop. Which one you like pass?" And the people are truly confused.

In a little nondescript coffee shop where I sometimes stop for a hamburger in Amherst there are some unfunny inscriptions hanging on the walls, representing a one-sided dialogue between management and staff. The unfunniest of them all reads—poetically:

> Take care of your boss
> The next one may be worse.

The trouble with writers is that they will often refuse to live by such rationality.

4

The Novelist as Teacher

WRITING OF THE KIND I DO is relatively new in my part of the world and it is too soon to try and describe in detail the complex of relationships between us and our readers. However, I think I can safely deal with one aspect of these relationships which is rarely mentioned. Because of our largely European education our writers may be pardoned if they begin by thinking that the relationship between European writers and their audience will automatically reproduce itself in Africa. We have learnt from Europe that a writer or an artist lives on the fringe of society—wearing a beard and a peculiar dress and generally behaving in a strange, unpredict-

First published in the *New Statesman*, London, January 29, 1965; subsequently in *Morning Yet on Creation Day*, Doubleday Anchor Books, 1975.

able way. He is in revolt against society, which in turn looks on him with suspicion if not hostility. The last thing society would dream of doing is to put him in charge of anything.

All that is well known, which is why some of us seem too eager for our society to treat us with the same hostility or even behave as though it already does. But I am not interested now in what writers expect of society; that is generally contained in their books, or should be. What is not so well documented is what society expects of its writers.

I am assuming, of course, that our writer and his society live in the same place. I realize that a lot has been made of the allegation that African writers have to write for European and American readers because African readers where they exist at all are only interested in reading textbooks. I don't know if African writers always have a foreign audience in mind. What I do know is that they don't have to. At least I know that I don't have to. Last year the pattern of sales of *Things Fall Apart* in the cheap paperback edition was as follows: about 800 copies in Britain; 20,000 in Nigeria; and about 2,500 in all other places. The same pattern was true also of *No Longer at Ease*.

Most of my readers are young. They are either in school or college or have only recently left. And many of them look to me as a kind of teacher. Only the other day I received this letter from Northern Nigeria:

Dear C. Achebe,

I do not usually write to authors, no matter how interesting their work is, but I feel I must tell you how much I enjoyed your editions of *Things Fall Apart* and *No Longer at Ease*. I look forward to reading your new edition *Arrow of God*. Your novels serve as advice to us young. I trust that you will continue to produce as many of this type of books. With friendly greetings and best wishes.

> Yours sincerely,
> I. BUBA YERO MAFINDI

It is quite clear what this particular reader expects of me. Nor is there much doubt about another reader in Ghana who wrote me a rather pathetic letter to say that I had neglected to include questions and answers at the end of *Things Fall Apart* and could I make these available to him to ensure his success at next year's school certificate examination. This is what I would call in Nigerian pidgin "a how-for-do" reader and I hope there are not very many like him. But also in Ghana I met a young woman teacher who immediately took me to task for not making the hero of my *No Longer at Ease* marry the girl he is in love with. I made the kind of vague noises I usually make whenever a wise critic comes along to tell me I should have written a different book to the one I wrote. But my woman teacher was not going to be shaken off so easily. She was in deadly earnest. Did I know, she said, that there were many women in the kind of situation I had described and that I could have served them well if I had shown that it was possible to find one man with enough guts to go against custom?

I don't agree, of course. But this young woman spoke with so much feeling that I couldn't help being a little uneasy at the accusation (for it was indeed a serious accusation) that I had squandered a rare opportunity for education on a whimsical and frivolous exercise. It is important to say at this point that no self-respecting writer will take dictation from his audience. He must remain free to disagree with his society and go into rebellion against it if need be. But I am for choosing my cause very carefully. Why should I start waging war as a Nigerian newspaper editor was doing the other day on the "soulless efficiency" of Europe's industrial and technological civilization when the very thing my society needs may well be a little technical efficiency?

My thinking on the peculiar needs of different societies was sharpened when not long ago I heard an English pop song which I think was entitled *"I Ain't Gonna Wash for a Week."* At first I wondered why it should occur to anyone to take such a vow when there were so many much more worthwhile resolutions to make. But later it dawned on me that this singer belonged to the same culture which in an earlier age of self-satisfaction had blasphemed and said that cleanliness was next to godliness. So I saw him in a new light —as a kind of divine administrator of vengeance. I make bold to say, however, that his particular offices would not be required in my society because we did not commit the sin of turning hygiene into a god.

Needless to say, we do have our own sins and blasphemies recorded against our name. If I were God I would regard as the very worst our acceptance—for whatever reason—of racial inferiority. It is too late in the day to get worked up about it or to blame others, much as they may deserve such blame and condemnation. What we need to do is to look back and try and find out where we went wrong, where the rain began to beat us.

Let me give one or two examples of the result of the disaster brought upon the African psyche in the period of subjection to alien races. I remember the shock felt by Christians of my father's generation in my village in the early 1940s when for the first time the local girls' school performed

Nigerian dances at the anniversary of the coming of the gospel. Hitherto they had always put on something Christian and civilized which I believe was called the Maypole dance. In those days—when I was growing up—I also remember that it was only the poor benighted heathen who had any use for our local handicraft, e.g., our pottery. Christians and the well-to-do (and they were usually the same people) displayed their tins and other metalware. We never carried water pots to the stream. I had a small cylindrical biscuit-tin suitable to my years while the older members of our household carried four-gallon kerosene tins.

Today, things have changed a lot, but it would be foolish to pretend that we have fully recovered from the traumatic effects of our first confrontation with Europe. Three or four weeks ago my wife, who teaches English in a boys' school, asked a pupil why he wrote about winter when he meant the harmattan. He said the other boys would call him a bushman if he did such a thing! Now, you wouldn't have thought, would you, that there was something shameful in your weather? But apparently we do. How can this great blasphemy be purged? I think it is part of my business as a writer to teach that boy that there is nothing disgraceful about the African weather, that the palm tree is a fit subject for poetry.

Here then is an adequate revolution for me to espouse—to help my society regain belief in itself and put away the complexes of the years of denigration and self-abasement. And it is essentially a question of education, in the best sense of that word. Here, I think, my aims and the deepest aspirations of my society meet. For no thinking African can escape the pain of the wound in our soul. You have all heard of the "African personality"; of African democracy, of the African way to socialism, of negritude, and so on. They are all props we have fashioned at different times to help us get on our feet again. Once we are up we shan't need any of them anymore. But for the moment it is in the nature of things that we may need to counter racism with what Jean-Paul Sartre has called an anti-racist racism, to announce not just that we are as good as the next man but that we are much better.

The writer cannot expect to be excused from the task of re-education and regeneration that must be done. In fact, he should march right in front. For he is, after all—as Ezekiel Mphahlele says in his *African Image*—the sensitive point of his community. The Ghanaian professor of philosophy, William Abraham, puts it this way:

> Just as African scientists undertake to solve some of the scientific problems of Africa, African historians go into the history of Africa, African political scientists concern themselves with the politics of Africa; why should African literary creators be exempted from the services that they themselves recognize as genuine?

I for one would not wish to be excused. I would be quite satisfied if my novels (especially the ones I set in the past) did no more than teach my readers that their past—with all its imperfections—was not one long night of savagery from which the first Europeans acting on God's behalf delivered them. Perhaps what I write is applied art as distinct from pure. But who cares? Art is important, but so is education of the kind I have in mind. And I don't see that the two need be mutually exclusive. In a recent anthology a Hausa folk tale, having recounted the usual fabulous incidents, ends with these words:

They all came and they lived happily together. He had several sons and daughters who grew up and helped in raising the standard of education of the country.[1]

As I said elsewhere, if you consider this ending a naïve anticlimax then you cannot know very much about Africa.

Leeds University, 1965

5

The Writer
and His Community

ONE OF THE MOST critical consequences of the transition from oral traditions to written forms of literature is the emergence of individual authorship.

The story told by the fireside does not belong to the story-teller once he has let it out of his mouth. But the story composed by his spiritual descendant, the writer in his study, "belongs" to its composer.

This shift is facilitated by the simple fact that, whereas a story that is told has no physical form or solidity, a book has; it is a commodity and can be handled and moved about. But I want to suggest that the physical form of a book cannot by

Originally given as the Regents' Lecture at the University of California at Los Angeles in November 1984.

itself adequately account for the emergent notion of proprietorship. At best it facilitates the will to ownership which is already present. This will is rooted in the praxis of individualism in its social and economic dimensions.

Part of my artistic and intellectual inheritance is derived from a cultural tradition in which it was possible for artists to create objects of art which were solid enough and yet make no attempt to claim, and sometimes even go to great lengths to deny, personal ownership of what they have created. I am referring to the tradition of *mbari* art in some parts of Igboland.

Mbari is an artistic "spectacular" demanded of the community by one or other of its primary divinities, usually the Earth goddess. To execute this "command performance" the community is represented by a small group of its members selected and secluded for months or even years for the sole purpose of erecting a befitting "home of images" filled to overflowing with sculptures and paintings in homage to the presiding god or goddess.

These representatives (called *ndimgbe;* sing.: *onyemgbe),* chosen to re-enact, as it were, the miracle of creation in its extravagant profusion, are always careful to disclaim all credit for making, which rightly belongs to gods; or even for initiating homage for what is made, which is the prerogative of the community. *Ndimgbe* are no more than vessels in which the gods place their gifts of creativity to mankind and in which the community afterwards make their token return of sacrifice and thanksgiving. As soon as their work is done behind the fence of their seclusion and they re-emerge into secular life, *ndimgbe* set about putting as much distance as possible between themselves and their recently executed works of art.

As Herbert Cole tells us in his study of this profound phenomenon:

> A former *onyemgbe* fears that he might slip up and say, "Look, I did this figure." If he [says] that, he has killed himself. The god that owns that work will kill him.[1]

This may sound strange and exotic to some ears, but I believe that it dramatizes a profoundly important aspect of the truth about art without which our understanding must remain seriously limited.

I am suggesting that what is at issue here is the principle which has come to be known as individualism and which has dominated the life and the psychology of the West in its modern history. The virtues of individualism are held to be universally beneficial but particularly so to the artist. John Plamenatz in his introduction to *Man and Society* separates the artist from the scholar in these words: "The artist ploughs his own furrow, the scholar, even in the privacy of his study, cultivates a common field."

It has been said that the American Ralph Waldo Emerson was perhaps the first to use the word "individualism" in the English language, rather approvingly, as a definition for the way of life which upholds the primacy of the individual. His definition was imbued with typically American optimistic faith. Emerson's contemporary, the Frenchman Alexis de Tocqueville, was far less enthusiastic. In his book *Democracy in America* he used "individualism" pejoratively—as a threat to society. As it turned out, however, it was the vision defined by Emerson that carried the day not just in America but in the Western world generally, from where it has made and continues to make serious inroads into the lives of other peoples.

The phenomenal success of the West in the mastery of the natural world is one of the dominant facts of modern history. It is only natural to attribute this dazzling achievement to the ruling values of the West, and also to hold these values up to the rest of the world not just as values but as the *right* values. By and large the rest of the world has been increasingly inclined to be persuaded. But from time to time, in life as in literature, voices of doubt have also been heard.

In a crucial passage in the novel *Ambiguous Adventure,* by the Senegalese Muslim writer Cheikh Hamidou Kane, the hero, an African student of philosophy in Paris, is asked by his dinner host how the history of Western thought strikes an African. And his reply—in my view one of the highlights of that fine novel—is as follows:

> It seems to me that this history has undergone an accident which has shifted it and, finally, drawn it away from its plan. Do you understand me? Socrates's scheme of thinking does not seem to me, at bottom, different from that of Saint Augustine though there was Christ between them. The plan is the same, as far as Pascal. It is still the plan of all the thought which is not occidental . . . I do not know. But don't you feel as if the philosophical plan were already no longer the same with Descartes as with Pascal? It is not the mystery which has changed but the questions which are asked of it and the revelations which are expected from it. Descartes is more niggardly in his quest. If, thanks to this and also to his method, he obtains a greater number of responses, what he reports also concerns us less and is of little help to us.[2]

It may be thought over-bold, if not downright impertinent, for anyone, but more particularly for an African student, to describe Descartes, the very father of modern Western philosophy, as the cause of a gigantic philosophical accident. But there are undoubtedly good grounds for the proposition advanced here that if they should return to the world today Socrates—or his student Plato, whom we know better—and Augustine might find African communalism more congenial than Western individualism. *The Republic,* "conjured out of the ruins of fourth-century Athens,"[3] was after all a grand design for the *ordering* of men in society; and *The City of God* a Christian reordering of society after the destruction of the Roman Empire by pagans. In other words, philosophy for Plato and Augustine, historically equidistant from Christ, was concerned with architectural designs for a better world.

Descartes, on the other hand, would probably become an American citizen if he should return. He had rejected the traditional contemplative ideal of philosophy and put in its place a new experimental rationalism and a mechanistic view of the physical world. He regarded science as a means of acquiring mastery over nature for the benefit of mankind and led the way himself with experiments in optics and physiology. But—and this perhaps more than all else makes him a true modern, Western man—he made the foundation of his philosophical edifice, including the existence of God, contingent on his own first person singular! *Cogito ergo sum.* I think therefore I am!

Perhaps it is the triumphant, breathtaking egocentrism of that declaration that occasionally troubles the non-Western mind, conscious as it must be of hierarchies above self; and so leads it to the brazen thought of a Western ontological accident.

But troubled though he may be, non-Western man is also, in spite of himself, dazzled by the technological marvels created by the West; by its ability to provide better than anybody else for man's material needs. And so we find him going out to meet the West in a bid to find out the secret of its astonishing success or, if that proves too rigorous, then simply to taste its fruits.

The philosophical dialogue between the West and Africa has rarely been better presented than in *Ambiguous Adventure.* In the first part of the story the proud rulers of the Diallobe people—bearers of the crescent of Islam in the West African savannah for close upon a thousand years—are suffering the traumatic anguish of defeat by French imperial arms, and pondering what the future course of their life should be. Should they send their children to the new French school or not? After a long and anguished debate they finally opt for the school but not on the admission that their own institutions are in any way inferior to those of the French, nor on the aspiration that they should become like the French in due course, but rather on the tactical grounds only that they must learn from their new masters "the art of conquering without being in the right."

The trouble with their decision, however, is that the children, these "wanderers on delicate feet" as the poet Senghor might have called them, these infant magi launched into an ambiguous journey with an ambivalent mandate to *experience* but not to *become,* are doomed from the start to distress and failure.

The hero of the novel, the deliverer-to-be and paragon of the new generation, returns from France a total spiritual wreck, his once vibrant sense of community hopelessly shattered. Summoned to assume the mantle of leadership, his tortured soul begs to be excused, to be left alone. "What have their problems to do with me?" he asks. "I am only myself. I have only me." Poor fellow; the West has got him!

Western literature played a central role in promoting the

ideal of individual autonomy. As Lionel Trilling pointed out, this literature has, in the last one hundred and fifty years, held "an intense and adverse imagination of the culture in which it has its being." It promoted the view of society and of culture as a prisonhouse from which the individual must escape in order to find space and fulfilment.

But fulfilment is not, as people often think, uncluttered space or an absence of controls, obligations, painstaking exertion. No! It is actually a presence—a powerful demanding presence limiting the space in which the self can roam uninhibited; it is an aspiration by the self to achieve spiritual congruence with the other.

When people speak glibly of fulfilment they often mean self-gratification, which is easy, short-lived and self-centred. Like drugs, it has to be experienced frequently, preferably in increasing doses.

Fulfilment is other-centred, a giving or subduing of the self, perhaps to somebody, perhaps to a cause; in any event to something external to it. Those who have experienced fulfilment all attest to the reality of this otherness. For religious people the soul of man aspires to God for fulfilment. St. Augustine, Bishop of Hippo in North Africa and one of the greatest fathers of the early Christian Church, understood this very well, having led a life of self-centred pleasure in his youth. He found fulfilment and left his great prayer in testimony: "For thyself hast thou made us, O God, and our heart is restless until it rests in Thee." Artists, scientists and scholars may find fulfilment in their creative work, humanitarians in their service. But even more important, ordinary men and women have found fulfilment in their closeness to others—to children, to parents, to wife or husband, to lover—and in social work of all kinds.

The French anthropologist O. Manoni wrote as follows about the Merina of Malagasy:

> We do not find in him that disharmony almost amounting to conflict between the social being and the inner personality which is so frequently met with among the civilized.[4]

We must note in passing, but not be diverted by, Manoni's typically occidentalist notion of civilization. The valuable part of his observation is that there is "disharmony almost amounting to conflict between the social being and the inner personality" in Western culture and, we may add, increasingly among its newly "civilized" and "civilizing" surrogates.

It was widely believed that this psychological disharmony, if not exactly desirable, was the inevitable price to be paid for the enormous advances made by the West in material wealth, in technology, in medicine, etc. Consequently the possibility that non-Western values might have insights to contribute to the process of modernization around the world was hardly even considered—until Japan.

In the area of literature, I recall that we have sometimes been informed by the West and its local zealots that the African novels we write are not novels at all because they do not quite fit the specifications of that literary form which came into being at a particular time in specific response to the new spirit of individual freedom set off by the decay of feudal Europe and the rise of capitalism. This form, we were told, was designed to explore individual rather than social predicaments.

As it happens the novel, even in its home of origin, has not behaved very well; it has always resisted the strait-jacket. What is more, being a robust art form, it has travelled indefatigably and picked up all kinds of strange habits!

Not so long ago the Czech writer Milan Kundera was reported as follows:

> The novel is an investigation into human existence . . . [It] proclaims no truth, no morality . . . That is a job for others: leaders of political parties, presidents, terrorists, priests, revolutionaries and editorial writers. The novel came about at the beginning of modern times when man was discovering how hard it is to get at the truth and how relative human affairs really are.[5]

I must confess I do like some things in that statement, not least his juxtaposition of presidents and terrorists, for when a president pursues a terrorist the two become quite indistinguishable! Nevertheless, I consider Kundera's position too Eurocentric, too dogmatic and therefore erroneous. If the novel came about in particular ways and circumstances, must it remain forever in the mould of its origin? If Europe discovered relativity in human affairs rather late, does it follow that everybody else did? And finally, can anyone seriously suggest that the novel proclaims no morality?

In the introduction to his book *Ninety-nine Novels—the Best in English Since 1939* the British novelist Anthony Burgess states—correctly in my opinion—that "the novel is what the symphony or painting or sculpture is not—namely a form steeped in morality."[6] Needless to say, Burgess is not talking about what he himself calls black-and-white, Sunday-sermon, conventional morality. "Rather," he says, "a novel will question convention and suggest to us that the making of moral judgements is difficult. This can be called the higher morality."[7]

And yet we cannot simply dismiss the desperate plea of Milan Kundera, an artist speaking out of the experience of an authoritarian state that arrogates to itself powers to define truth and morality for the writer. No! We must recognize his special exigencies or, as he himself says, "how relative human affairs really are." Or, as Burgess says, "that the making of moral judgements is difficult."

We may have been talking about individualism as if it was invented in the West or even by one American, Emerson. In fact, individualism must be, has to be, as old as human society itself. From whatever time humans began to move around in groups the dialogue between Manoni's polarities of "social being" and "inner personality" or, more simply, between the individual and the community must also have been called into being. It is inconceivable that it shouldn't. The question then is not whether this dialectic has always existed but rather how particular peoples resolved it at particular times.

One of mankind's oldest written records, the Old Testament, has a fine and dramatic moment when the prophet Ezekiel proposes to his people a shift in dealing with the old paradox. "The soul that sinneth, it shall die," he says, superseding in that bold declaration the teaching that when fathers eat sour grapes their children's teeth are set on edge.

Some years ago, John Updike after he had finished reading my *Arrow of God* wrote me a letter in which he made some interesting observations. I'd like to quote a paragraph from that letter because it has an interesting bearing on what I have been trying to say:

> The final developments of *Arrow of God* proved unexpected and, as I think about them, beautifully resonant, tragic and theological. That Ezeulu, whom we had seen stand up so invincibly to both Nwaka and Clarke, should be so suddenly vanquished by his own god Ulu and by something harsh and vengeful within himself, and his defeat in a page or two be the fulcrum of a Christian lever upon his people, is an ending few Western novelists would have contrived; having created a

hero they would not let him crumble, nor are they, by and large, as truthful as you in their witness to the cruel reality of process.

Of course a Westerner would be most reluctant to destroy "in a page or two" the very angel and paragon of creation—the individual hero. If indeed he has to be destroyed, it must be done expansively with detailed explanations and justifications, not to talk of lamentations. And he must be given as final tribute the limelight in which to speak a grand, valedictory soliloquy!

The non-Westerner does not as a rule have those obligations because in his traditional scheme and hierarchy the human hero does not loom so large. Even when, like Ezeulu, he is leader and priest, he is still in a very real sense subordinate to his community. But even more important, he is subject to the sway of non-human forces in the universe, call them God, Fate, Chance or what you will. I call them sometimes the Powers of Event, the repositories of causes and wisdoms that are as yet, and perhaps will always be, inaccessible to us.

To powers inhabiting that order of reality the human hero counts for little. If they should desire his fall they will not be obliged to make a long-winded case or present explanations.

Does this mean then that among these people, the Igbo to take one example, the individual counts for nothing? Paradoxical as it may sound the answer is an emphatic "No." The Igbo are second to none in their respect of the individual personality. For whereas many cultures are content to demonstrate the value and importance of each man and woman by reference to the common fatherhood of God, the Igbo postulate an unprecedented uniqueness for the individual by making him or her the sole creation and purpose of a unique god-agent, *chi*. No two persons, not even blood brothers, are created and accompanied by the same *chi*.

And yet the Igbo people as we have seen immediately set about balancing this extraordinary specialness, this unsurpassed individuality, by setting limits to its expression. The first limit is the democratic one, which subordinates the person to the group in practical, social matters. And the other is a moral taboo on excess, which sets a limit to personal ambition, surrounding it with powerful cautionary tales.

I began by describing—all too briefly—an aspect of the question of the "ownership" of art among a major Igbo group. I will end by quoting what an American anthropologist, Simon Ottenberg, reported about another group. He is describing an Afikpo carver at work on ritual masks:

> Sometimes his friends or other secret society members hear him working in the bush, so they come and sit with him and watch him carve. They give him advice telling him how to carve, even if they themselves do not know how. He is not offended by their suggestions . . . I felt myself that he rather enjoyed the company.[8]

Clearly, this artist and his people are in very close communion. They do not all have to agree on how to make the best mask. But they are all interested in the process of making and the final outcome. The resulting art is important because it is at the centre of the life of the people and so can fulfil some of that need that first led man to make art: the need to afford himself through his imagination an alternative handle on reality.

There is always a grave danger of oversimplification in any effort to identify differences between systems such as I have attempted here between "The West and the Rest of Us," to borrow the catchy title of Chinweizu's remarkable book.[9] I hope that while drawing attention to peculiarities which, in my view, are real enough at this point in time I have not fallen, nor led my indulgent reader, into the trap of seeing the differences as absolute rather than relative. But to be completely sure let me restate that the testimony of John Updike and certainly of Anthony Burgess does not encourage the notion of an absolute dichotomy between the West and ourselves on the issues I have been dealing with.

And I should like to go further and call to testimony a very distinguished witness indeed—J. B. Priestley—who wrote in a famous essay, "Literature and Western Man," as follows:

> Characters in a society make the novel . . . Society itself becomes more and more important to the serious novelist, and indeed turns into a character itself, perhaps the chief character.[10]

Priestley could be speaking here more about the fictional use a novelist might make of his society rather than the real-life relationship between them. But in either case the level of understanding of, and even identification with, society he implicitly demands of the writer is a far cry from the adversary relationship generally assumed and promoted in the West.

The final point I wish to address myself to is the crucial one of identity. Who is my community? The *mbari* and the Afikpo examples I referred to were clearly appropriate to the rather small, reasonably stable and self-contained societies to which they belonged. In the very different, wide-open, multicultural and highly volatile condition known as modern Nigeria, for example, can a writer even begin to know who his community is let alone devise strategies for relating to it?

If I write novels in a country in which most citizens are

illiterate, who then is my community? If I write in English in a country in which English may still be called a foreign language, or in any case is spoken only by a minority, what use is my writing?

These are clearly grave issues. And it is not surprising that very many thoughtful people have exercised their minds in seeking acceptable answers. Neither is it surprising that less serious people should be handy with an assortment of instant and painless cures.

To the question of writing at all we have sometimes been counselled to forget it, or rather the writing of books. What is required, we are told, is plays and films. Books are out of date! The book is dead, long live television! One question which is not even raised let alone considered is: Who will write the drama and film scripts when the generation that can read and write has been used up?

On language we are given equally simplistic prescriptions. Abolish the use of English! But after its abolition we remain seriously divided on what to put in its place. One proffered solution gives up Nigeria with its 200-odd languages as a bad case and travels all the way to East Africa to borrow Swahili; just as in the past a kingdom caught in a succession bind sometimes solved its problem by going to another kingdom to hire an underemployed prince!

I will not proceed with these fancy answers to deeply profound problems. To those colleagues who might be tempted into a hasty switch of genres I will say this: Consider a hypothetical case. A master singer arrives to perform in a large auditorium and finds at the last moment that three-quarters of his audience are totally deaf. His sponsors then put the proposition to him that he should dance instead because even the deaf can *see* a dancer. Now, although our performer may have the voice of an angel his feet are as heavy as concrete. So what should he do? Should he proceed to sing beautifully to only a quarter or less of the auditorium or dance atrociously to a full house?

I guess it is clear where my stand would be! The singer should sing well even if it is merely to himself, rather than dance badly for the whole world. This is, of course, putting the case in its utmost extremity; but it becomes necessary to do it in defence of both art and good sense in the face of what I see as a new onslaught of barbaric simple-mindedness.

Fortunately, in real life, we are not in danger of these bizarre extremes unless we consciously work our way into them. I can see no situation in which I will be presented with a Draconic choice between reading books and watching movies; or between English and Igbo. For me, no either/or; I insist on both. Which, you might say, makes my life rather difficult and even a little untidy. But I prefer it that way.

Despite the daunting problems of identity that beset our contemporary society, we can see in the horizon the beginnings of a new relationship between artist and community which will not flourish like the mango-trick in the twinkling of an eye but will rather, in the hard and bitter manner of David Diop's young tree, grow patiently and obstinately to the ultimate victory of liberty and fruition.

6

The Igbo World
and Its Art

THE IGBO WORLD is an arena for the interplay of forces. It is a dynamic world of movement and of flux. Igbo art, reflecting this world-view, is never tranquil but mobile and active, even aggressive.

Ike, energy, is the essence of all things human, spiritual, animate and inanimate. Everything has its own unique energy which must be acknowledged and given its due. *Ike di na awaja na awaja* is a common formulation of this idea: "Power runs in many channels." Sometimes the saying is extended by an exemplifying coda about a mild and gentle

Originally published as Foreword to *Igbo Arts: Community and Cosmos* by Herbert M. Cole and Chike C. Aniakor, Museum of Cultural History, University of California at Los Angeles, 1984.

bird, *obu,* which nonetheless possesses the power to destroy a
snake. *Onye na nkie, onye na nkie*—literally, "everyone and
his own"—is a social expression of the same notion often
employed as a convenient formula for saluting *en masse* an
assembly too large for individual greetings.

In some cultures a person may worship one of the gods or
goddesses in the pantheon and pay scant attention to the rest.
In Igbo religion such selectiveness is unthinkable. All the
people must placate all the gods all the time! For there is a
cautionary proverb which states that even when a person has
satisfied the deity Udo completely he may yet be killed by
Ogwugwu. The degree of peril propounded by this proverb
is only dimly apprehended until one realizes that Ogwugwu
is not a stranger to Udo but his very consort!

It is the striving to come to terms with a multitude of
forces and demands which gives Igbo life its tense and restless dynamism and its art an outward, social and kinetic
quality. But it would be a mistake to take the extreme view
that Igbo art has no room for contemplative privacy. In the
first place, all extremism is abhorrent to the Igbo sensibility;
but specifically, the Igbo word which is closest to the English
word "art" is *nka,* and Igbo people do say: *Onye nakwa nka
na-eme ka ona-adu iru,* which means that an artist at work is
apt to wear an unfriendly face. In other words, he is excused
from the normal demands of sociability! If further proof is
required of this need for privacy in the creative process, it is
provided clearly and definitively in the ritual seclusion of the
makers of *mbari,* to which we shall return shortly.

But once made, art emerges from privacy into the public
domain. There are no private collections among the Igbo
beyond personal ritual objects like the *ikenga.* Indeed, the
very concept of collections would be antithetical to the Igbo

artistic intention. Collections by their very nature will impose rigid, artistic attitudes and conventions on creativity which the Igbo sensibility goes out of its way to avoid. The purposeful neglect of the painstakingly and devoutly accomplished *mbari* houses with all the art objects in them, as soon as the primary mandate of their creation has been served, provides a significant insight into the Igbo aesthetic value as process rather than product. Process is motion while product is rest. When the product is preserved or venerated, the impulse to repeat the process is compromised. Therefore the Igbo choose to eliminate the product and retain the process so that every occasion and every generation will receive its own impulse and kinesis of creation. Interestingly, this aesthetic disposition receives powerful endorsement from the tropical climate which provides an abundance of materials for making art, such as wood, as well as formidable enemies of stasis, such as humidity and the termite. Visitors to Igboland are often shocked to see that artefacts are rarely accorded any particular value on account of age alone.

In popular contemporary usage the Igbo formulate their view of the world as: "No condition is permanent." In Igbo cosmology even gods could fall out of use; and new forces are liable to appear without warning in the temporal and metaphysical firmament. The practical purpose of art is to channel a spiritual force into an aesthetically satisfying physical form that captures the presumed attributes of that force. It stands to reason, therefore, that new forms must stand ready to be called into being as often as new (threatening) forces appear on the scene. It is like "earthing" an electrical charge to ensure communal safety.

The frequent representation of the alien district officer among traditional *mbari* figures is an excellent example of the mediating role of art between old and new, between accepted norms and extravagant aberrations. Art must interpret all human experience, for anything against which the door is barred can cause trouble. Even if harmony is not achievable in the heterogeneity of human experience, the dangers of an open rupture are greatly lessened by giving to everyone his due in the same forum of social and cultural surveillance. The alien district officer may not, after all, be a greater oddity than a local woman depicted in the act of copulating with a dog, and such powerful aberrations must be accorded tactful artistic welcome-cum-invigilation.

Of all the art forms, the dance and the masquerade would appear to have satisfied the Igbo artistic appetite most completely. If the masquerade were not limited to the male sex alone, one might indeed call it the art form *par excellence* for it subsumes not only the dance but all other forms—sculpture, music, painting, drama, costumery, even architecture, for the Ijele masquerade is indeed a most fabulously extravagant construction.

What makes the dance and the masquerade so satisfying to the Igbo disposition is, I think, their artistic deployment of motion, of agility, which informs the Igbo concept of existence. The masquerade (which is really an elaborated dance) not only moves spectacularly but those who want to enjoy its motion fully must follow its progress up and down the arena. This seemingly minor observation was nonetheless esteemed important enough by the Igbo to be elevated into a proverb of general application: *Ada-akwu ofu ebe enene mmuo,* "You do not stand in one place to watch a masquerade." You must imitate its motion. The kinetic energy of the masquerade's art is thus instantly transmitted to a whole arena of spectators.

So potent is motion stylized into dance that the Igbo have sought to defeat with its power even the final immobility of death by contriving a funeral rite in which the bearers of the corpse perform the *abia* dance with their burden, transforming by their motion the body's imminent commitment to earth into an active rite of passage.

This body, appropriately transfigured, will return on festival or ritual occasions or during serious social crises, as a masquerade to participate with an enhanced presence and authority in the affairs of the community, speaking an esoteric dialect in which people are referred to as bodies: "The body of so-and-so, I salute you!"

Masquerades are of many kinds representing the range of human experience—from youth to age; from playfulness to terror; from the delicate beauty of the maiden spirit, *agbogho mmuo,* to the candid ugliness of *njo ka-oya,* "ugliness greater than disease"; from the athleticism of *ogolo* to the legless and armless inertia of *ebu-ebu,* a loquacious masquerade that has to be carried from place to place on the head of its attendant from which position it is wont to shout: Off we go! *(Ije abulu ufia!);* from masquerades that appear at every festival to the awesome ancestors that are enticed to the world by rare crises such as the desecration of a masked spirit; from the vast majority that appear in daytime to the dreaded invisible chorus, *ayaka,* and the night-runner, *ogbazulobodo.*

I hasten to add that the examples given above are merely localized impressionistic illustrations taken from my own experience of growing up in Ogidi in the 1930s and 1940s. There are variations from one village community to the next and certainly from one region of Igboland to another. Nothing here can do justice, for instance, to the extraordinary twin traditions of Odo and Omabe of the Nsukka region. To encounter an Omabe masquerade just descended from the hills for a brief sojourn in the world after an absence of three years, its body of tiny metal discs throwing back the dying lights of dusk, can be a truly breathtaking experience!

The awesomeness of masquerades has suffered in modern times. This is not due, as some imagine, to the explosion of the secret concerning what lies behind the mask. Even in the past the women merely pretended not to know! I remember as a child a masquerade whose name was *Omanu kwue*— meaning, "If you know, speak." This was a dare, of course, and nobody was about to take up the challenge. But this masquerade was of such towering height that there was only one man in the whole of Ogidi, perhaps even in the whole world, who could carry it; the same man, incidentally, whose brief career as a policeman at the beginning of the century had left a powerful enough legend for him to be represented in his uniform in an *mbari* house in faraway Owerri and simply called Ogidi.

In the past, knowing who walked within the mask did not detract from the numinous, dramatic presence of a representative of the ancestors on a brief mission to the living. Disbelief was easily suspended! The decline today is merely a symptom of the collapse of a whole eschatology. But at least in my dreams masquerades have not ceased to bring forth the panic terror of childhood.

7

Colonialist Criticism

THE WORD "colonialist" may be deemed inappropriate for two reasons. First, it has come to be associated in many minds with that brand of cheap, demagogic and outmoded rhetoric which the distinguished Ghanaian public servant Robert Gardiner no doubt has in mind when he speaks of our tendency to "intone the colonial litany," implying that the time has come when we must assume responsibility for our problems and our situation in the world and resist the temptation to blame other people. Secondly, it may be said

This essay is based on a paper read to the Association for Commonwealth Literature and Language Studies at Makerere University, Uganda, in January 1974; later published in *Morning Yet on Creation Day*, Doubleday Anchor Books, 1975.

that whatever colonialism may have done in the past, the very fact of a Commonwealth Conference today is sufficient repudiation of it, is indeed a symbol of a new relationship of equality between peoples who were once masters and servants.

Yet in spite of the strength of these arguments one feels the necessity to deal with some basic issues raised by a certain specious criticism which flourishes in African literature today and which derives from the same basic attitude and assumption as colonialism itself and so merits the name "colonialist." This attitude and assumption was crystallized in Albert Schweitzer's immortal dictum in the heyday of colonialism: "The African is indeed my brother, but my junior brother." The latter-day colonialist critic, equally given to big-brother arrogance, sees the African writer as a somewhat unfinished European who with patient guidance will grow up one day and write like every other European, but meanwhile must be humble, must learn all he can and while at it give due credit to his teachers in the form of either direct praise or, even better since praise sometimes goes bad and becomes embarrassing, manifest self-contempt. Because of the tricky nature of this subject, I have chosen to speak not in general terms but wherever possible specifically about my own actual experience. In any case, as anyone who has heard anything at all about me may know already, I do have problems with universality and other concepts of that scope, being very much a down-to-earth person. But I will hope by reference to a few other writers and critics to show that my concerns and anxieties are perhaps not entirely personal.

When my first novel was published in 1958, a very unusual review of it was written by a British woman, Honor Tracy, who is perhaps not so much a critic as a literary journalist.

But what she said was so intriguing that I have never forgotten it. If I remember rightly, she headlined it "Three cheers for mere Anarchy!" The burden of the review itself was as follows: These bright Negro barristers (how barristers came into it remains a mystery to me to this day, but I have sometimes woven fantasies about an earnest white woman and an unscrupulous black barrister) who talk so glibly about African culture, how would they like to return to wearing raffia skirts? How would novelist Achebe like to go back to the mindless times of his grandfather instead of holding the modern job he has in broadcasting in Lagos?

I should perhaps point out that colonialist criticism is not always as crude as this, but the exaggerated grossness of a particular example may sometimes prove useful in studying the anatomy of the species. There are three principal parts here: Africa's inglorious past (raffia skirts) to which Europe brings the blessing of civilization (Achebe's modern job in Lagos) and for which Africa returns ingratitude (sceptical novels like *Things Fall Apart*).

Before I go on to more advanced varieties I must give one more example of the same kind as Honor Tracy's, which on account of its recentness (1970) actually surprised me:

> The British administration not only safeguarded women from the worst tyrannies of their masters, it also enabled them to make their long journeys to farm or market without armed guard, secure from the menace of hostile neighbours . . . The Nigerian novelists who have written the charming and bucolic accounts of domestic harmony in African rural communities, are the sons whom the labours of these women educated; the peaceful village of their childhood to which they nostalgically look back was one which had been purged of bloodshed and alcoholism by an ague-ridden district officer and a Scottish mission lassie whose years were cut short by every kind of intestinal parasite.

It is even true to say that one of the most nostalgically convincing of the rural African novelists used as his sourcebook not the memories of his grandfathers but the records of the despised British anthropologists . . . The modern African myth-maker hands down a vision of colonial rule in which the native powers are chivalrously viewed through the eyes of the hard-won liberal tradition of the late Victorian scholar, while the expatriates are shown as schoolboys' blackboard caricatures.[1]

I have quoted this at such length because first of all I am intrigued by Iris Andreski's literary style, which recalls so faithfully the sedate prose of the district officer government anthropologist of sixty or seventy years ago—a tribute to her remarkable powers of identification as well as to the durability of colonialist rhetoric. "Tyrannies of their masters" . . . "menace of hostile neighbours" . . . "purged of bloodshed and alcoholism." But in addition to this, Iris Andreski advances the position taken by Honor Tracy in one significant and crucial direction—its claim to a deeper knowledge and a more reliable appraisal of Africa than the educated African writer has shown himself capable of.

To the colonialist mind it was always of the utmost importance to be able to say: "I know my natives," a claim which implied two things at once: (a) that the native was really quite simple and (b) that understanding him and controlling him went hand in hand—understanding being a pre-condition for control and control constituting adequate proof of understanding. Thus, in the heyday of colonialism any serious incident of native unrest, carrying as it did disquieting intimations of slipping control, was an occasion not only for pacification by the soldiers but also (afterwards) for a royal commission of inquiry—a grand name for yet another perfunctory study of native psychology and institutions. Meanwhile a new situation was slowly developing as a handful of natives began to acquire European education and then to challenge Europe's presence and position in their native land with the intellectual weapons of Europe itself. To deal with this phenomenal presumption the colonialist devised two contradictory arguments. He created the "man of two worlds" theory to prove that no matter how much the native was exposed to European influences he could never truly absorb them; like Prester John he would always discard the mask of civilization when the crucial hour came and reveal his true face. Now, did this mean that the educated native was no different at all from his brothers in the bush? Oh, no! He *was* different; he was worse. His abortive effort at education and culture though leaving him totally unredeemed and unregenerated had nonetheless done something to him—it had deprived him of his links with his own people whom he no longer even understood and who certainly wanted none of his dissatisfaction or pretensions. "I know my natives; they are delighted with the way things are. It's only these half-educated ruffians who don't even know their own people . . ." How often one heard that and the many variations of it in colonial times! And how almost amusing to find its legacy in the colonialist criticism of our literature today! Iris Andreski's book is more than old wives' tales, at least in intention. It is clearly inspired by the desire to undercut the educated African witness (the modern myth-maker, she calls him) by appealing direct to the unspoilt woman of the bush who has retained a healthy gratitude for Europe's intervention in Africa. This desire accounts for all that reliance one finds in modern European travellers' tales on the evidence of "simple natives"—houseboys, cooks, drivers, schoolchildren —supposedly more trustworthy than the smart alecs. An American critic, Charles Larson, makes good use of this kind of evidence not only to validate his literary opinion of Ghana's Ayi Kwei Armah but, even more important, to demonstrate its superiority over the opinion of Ghanaian intellectuals:

> When I asked a number of students at the University of Ghana about their preferences for contemporary African novelists, Ayi Kwei Armah was the writer mentioned most frequently, in spite of the fact that many of Ghana's older writers and intellectuals regard him as a kind of negativist . . . I have for some time regarded Ayi Kwei Armah as Anglophone Africa's most accomplished prose stylist.[2]

In 1962, I published an essay, "Where Angels Fear to Tread,"[3] in which I suggested that the European critic of African literature must cultivate the habit of humility appropriate to his limited experience of the African world and purged of the superiority and arrogance which history so insidiously makes him heir to. That article, though couched in very moderate terms, won for me quite a few bitter enemies. One of them took my comments so badly—almost as a personal affront—that he launched numerous unprovoked attacks against me. Well, he has recently come to grief by his own hand. He published a long abstruse treatise based on an analysis of a number of Igbo proverbs most of which, it turned out, he had so completely misunderstood as to translate "fruit" in one of them as "penis." Whereupon, a merciless native, less charitable than I, proceeded to make mincemeat of him. If only he had listened to me ten years ago!

After the publication of *A Man of the People* in 1966, I was invited to dinner by a British diplomat in Lagos at which his wife, hitherto a fan of mine, admonished me for what she called "this great disservice to Nigeria." She loved Nigeria so much that my criticisms of the country which ignored all the brave efforts it was making left her totally aghast. I told her something not very nice, and our friendship was brought to an end.

Most African writers write out of an African experience and of commitment to an African destiny. For them, that destiny does not include a future European identity for which the present is but an apprenticeship. And let no one be fooled by the fact that we may write in English, for we intend to do unheard of things with it. Already some people are getting worried. This past summer I met one of Australia's leading poets, A. D. Hope, in Canberra, and he said wistfully that the only happy writers today were those writing in small languages like Danish. Why? Because they and their readers understood one another and knew precisely what a word meant when it was used. I had to admit that I hadn't thought of it that way. I had always assumed that the Commonwealth of Nations was a great bonus for a writer, that the English-Speaking Union was a desirable fraternity. But talking with A. D. Hope that evening, I felt somewhat like an illegitimate child face to face with the true son of the house lamenting the excesses of an adventurous and profligate father who had kept a mistress in every port. I felt momentarily nasty and thought of telling A. D. Hope: You ain't seen nothin' yet! But I know he would not have understood. And in any case, there was an important sense in which he was right—that every literature must seek the things that belong unto its peace, must, in other words, speak of a particular place, evolve out of the necessities of its history, past and current, and the aspirations and destiny of its people.

Australia proved quite enlightening. (I hope I do not sound too ungracious. Certainly, I met very many fine and sensitive people in Australia; and the words which the distinguished historian Professor Manning Clark wrote to me after my visit are among the finest tributes I have ever received: "I hope you come back and speak again here, because we need to lose the blinkers of our past. So come and help the young to grow up without the prejudices of their forefathers. . . ."

On another occasion a student at the National University who had taken a course in African literature asked me if the time had not come for African writers to write about "people in general" instead of just Africans. I asked her if by "people in general" she meant *like Australians,* and gave her the bad news that as far as I was concerned such a time would never come. She was only a brash sophomore. But like all the other women I have referred to, she expressed herself with passionate and disarming effrontery. I don't know how women's lib will take it, but I do believe that by and large women are more honest than men in expressing their feelings. This girl was only making the same point which many "serious" critics have been making more tactfully and therefore more insidiously. They dress it up in fine robes which they call universality.

In his book *The Emergence of African Fiction,* Charles Larson tells us a few revealing things about universality. In a chapter devoted to Lenrie Peters's novel, which he finds particularly impressive, he speaks of "its universality, its very limited concern with Africa itself." Then he goes on to spell it all out:

> That it is set in Africa appears to be accidental, for, except for a few comments at the beginning, Peters's story might just as easily take place in the southern part of the United States or in the southern regions of France or Italy. If a few names of characters and places were

changed one would indeed feel that this was an American novel. In short, Peters's story is universal.[4]

But Larson is obviously not as foolish as this passage would make him out to be, for he ends it on a note of self-doubt which I find totally disarming. He says (p. 238):

> Or am I deluding myself in considering the work universal? Maybe what I really mean is that *The Second Round* is to a great degree Western and therefore scarcely African at all.

I find it hard after that to show more harshness than merely agreeing about his delusion. But few people I know are prepared to be so charitable. In a recent review of the book in *Okike,* a Nigerian critic, Omolara Leslie, mocks "the shining faith that we are all Americans under the skin."

Does it ever occur to these universalists to try out their game of changing names of characters and places in an American novel, say, a Philip Roth or an Updike, and slotting in African names just to see how it works? But of course it would not occur to them. It would never occur to them to doubt the universality of their own literature. In the nature of things the work of a Western writer is automatically informed by universality. It is only others who must strain to achieve it. So-and-so's work is universal; he has truly arrived! As though universality were some distant bend in the road which you may take if you travel out far enough in the direction of Europe or America, if you put adequate distance between yourself and your home. I should like to see the word "universal" banned altogether from discussions of African literature until such a time as people cease to use it as a synonym for the narrow, self-serving parochialism of Europe, until their horizon extends to include all the world.

If colonialist criticism were merely irritating one might doubt the justification of devoting a whole essay to it. But strange though it may sound, some of its ideas and precepts do exert an influence on our writers, for it is a fact of our contemporary world that Europe's powers of persuasion can be far in excess of the merit and value of her case. Take for instance the black writer who seizes on the theme that "Africa's past is a sadly inglorious one" as though it were something new that had not already been "proved" adequately for him. Colonialist critics will, of course, fall all over him in ecstatic and salivating admiration—which is neither unexpected nor particularly interesting. What is fascinating, however, is the tortuous logic and sophistry they will sometimes weave around a perfectly straightforward and natural enthusiasm.

A review of Yambo Ouologuem's *Bound to Violence* (Heinemann Educational Books, London, 1971) by a Philip M. Allen in the *Pan-African Journal*[5] was an excellent example of sophisticated, even brilliant colonialist criticism. The opening sentence alone would reward long and careful examination; but I shall content myself here with merely quoting it:

> The achievement of Ouologuem's much discussed, impressive, yet over-praised novel has less to do with whose ideological team he's playing on than with the *forcing of moral universality on African civilization* [my italics].

A little later Mr. Allen expounds on this new moral universality:

> This morality is not only "un-African"—denying the standards set by omnipresent ancestors, the solidarity of communities, the legitimacy of social contract: it is a Hobbesian universe that extends beyond the

wilderness, beyond the white man's myths of Africa, into all civilization, theirs and ours.

If you should still be wondering at this point how Ouologuem was able to accomplish that Herculean feat of forcing moral universality on Africa or with what gargantuan tools, Mr. Allen does not leave you too long in suspense. Ouologuem is "an African intellectual who has mastered both a style and a prevailing philosophy of French letters," able to enter "the remoter alcoves of French philosophical discourse."

Mr. Allen is quite abrupt in dismissing all the "various polemical factions" and ideologists who have been claiming Ouologuem for their side. Of course they all miss the point,

> . . . for Ouologuem isn't writing their novel. He gives us an Africa cured of the pathetic obsession with racial and cultural confrontation and freed from invidious tradition-mongering . . . His book knows no easy antithesis between white and black, western and indigenous, modern and traditional. Its conflicts are those of the universe, not accidents of history.

And in final demonstration of Ouologuem's liberation from the constraint of local models Mr. Allen tells us:

> Ouologuem does not accept Fanon's idea of liberation, and he calls African unity a theory for dreamers. His Nakem is no more the Mali of Modibo Keita or the continent of Nkrumah than is the golden peace of Emperor Sundiata or the moral parish of Muntu.

Mr. Allen's rhetoric does not entirely conceal whose ideological team *he* is playing on, his attitude to Africa, in other words. Note, for example, the significant antithesis between the infinite space of "a Hobbesian universe" and "the moral parish of Muntu" with its claustrophobic implications. Who but Western man could contrive such arrogance?

Running through Mr. Allen's review is the overriding thesis that Ouologuem has somehow restored dignity to his people and their history by investing them with responsibility for violence and evil. Mr. Allen returns to this thesis again and again, merely changing the form of words. And we are to understand, by fairly clear implication, that this was something brave and new for Africa, this manly assumption of responsibility.

Of course a good deal of colonialist rhetoric always turned on that very question. The moral inferiority of colonized peoples, of which subjugation was a prime consequence and penalty, was most clearly demonstrated in their unwillingness to assume roles of responsibility. As long ago (or as recently, depending on one's historical perspective) as 1910 the popular English novelist John Buchan wrote a colonialist classic, *Prester John,* in which we find the words: "That is the difference between white and black, the gift of responsibility." And the idea did not originate with Buchan, either. It was a foundation tenet of colonialism and a recurrent element of its ideology and rhetoric. Now, to tell a man that he is incapable of assuming responsibility for himself and his actions is of course the utmost insult, to avoid which some Africans will go to any length, will throw anything into the deal; they will agree, for instance, to ignore the presence and role of racism in African history or pretend that somehow it was all the black man's own fault. Which is complete and utter nonsense. For whatever faults the black man may have or whatever crimes he committed (and they were, and are, legion) he did not bring racism into the world. And no matter how emancipated a man may wish to appear or how anxious to please by his largeness of heart, he cannot make history simply go away. Not even a brilliant writer could hope to do that. And as for those who applaud him for trying, who acclaim his bold originality in "restoring historical initiative to his people" when in reality all he does is pander to their racist and colonialist attitudes, they are no more than unscrupulous interrogators taking advantage of an ingratiating defendant's weakness and trust to egg him on to irretrievable self-incrimination.

That a "critic" playing on the ideological team of colonialism should feel sick and tired of Africa's "pathetic obsession with racial and cultural confrontation" should surprise no one. Neither should his enthusiasm for those African works that show "no easy antithesis between white and black." But an African who falls for such nonsense, not only in spite of Africa's so very recent history but, even more, in the face of continuing atrocities committed against millions of Africans in their own land by racist minority regimes, deserves a lot of pity. Certainly anyone, white or black, who chooses to see violence as the abiding principle of African civilization is free to do so. But let him not pass himself off as a restorer of dignity to Africa, or attempt to make out that he is writing about man and about the state of civilization in general. (You could as well claim that fifty years ago Frank Melland's *In Witchbound Africa* was an account of the universality of witchcraft and a vindication of Africa.) The futility of such service to Africa, leaving aside any question of duplicity in the motive, should be sufficiently underscored by one interesting admission in Mr. Allen's review:

> Thus, there is no reason for western reviewers of this book to exult in a black writer's admission of the savagery, sensuality and amorality of his

race: he isn't talking about his race as Senghor or Cleaver do: he's talking about us all.

Well, how obtuse of these "western reviewers" to miss that point and draw such wrong conclusions! But the trouble is that not everyone can be as bright as Mr. Allen. Perhaps for most ordinary people what Africa needs is a far less complicated act of restoration. The Canadian novelist and critic Margaret Laurence saw this happening already in the way many African writers are interpreting their world, making it

> . . . neither idyllic, as the views of some nationalists would have had it, nor barbaric, as the missionaries and European administrators wished and needed to believe.[6]

And in the epilogue to the same book she makes the point even more strongly:

> No writer of any quality has viewed the old Africa in an idealized way, but they have tried to regain what is rightly theirs—a past composed of real and vulnerable people, their ancestors, not the figments of missionary and colonialist imaginations.

Ultimately the question of ideological sides which Mr. Allen threw in only to dismiss it again with contempt may not be as far-fetched as he thinks. For colonialism itself was built also on an ideology (although its adherents may no longer realize it) which, despite many setbacks, survives into our own day, and indeed is ready again at the end of a quiescent phase of self-doubt for a new resurgence of proselytization, even, as in the past, among its prime victims!

Fortunately, it can no longer hope for the role of unchallenged arbiter in other people's affairs that it once took so much for granted. There are clear signs that critics and readers from those areas of the world where continuing incidents and recent memories of racism, colonialism and other forms of victimization exist will more and more demand to know from their writers just on whose ideological side they are playing. And we writers had better be prepared to reckon with this questioning. For no amount of prestige or laurels of metropolitan reputation would seem large enough to silence or overawe it. Consider, for instance, a recent judgement on V. S. Naipaul by a fellow Caribbean, Ivan Van Sertima:

> His brilliancy of wit I do not deny but, in my opinion, he has been overrated by English critics whose sensibilities he insidiously flatters by his stock-in-trade: self-contempt.[7]

A Nigerian, Ime Ikiddeh, was even less ceremonious in his dismissal of Naipaul, who he thought did not deserve the attention paid to him by Ngũgĩ wa Thiong'o in his *Home-coming*.[8] One need not accept these judgements in order to see them as signs of things to come.

Meanwhile the seduction of our writers by the blandishments of colonialist criticism is matched by its misdirection of our critics. Thus, an intelligent man like Dr. Sunday Anozie, the Nigerian scholar and critic, is able to dismiss the high moral and social earnestness sometimes expressed by one of our greatest poets, Christopher Okigbo, as only a mark of underdevelopment. In his book *Christopher Okigbo,* the most extensive biographical and critical study of the poet to date, Dr. Anozie tells us of Okigbo's "passion for truth," which apparently makes him sometimes too outspoken, makes him the talkative weaverbird "incapable of whispered secrets." And he proceeds to offer the following explanation:

> No doubt the thrill of actualized prophecy can sometimes lead poets particularly in the young countries to confuse their role with that of

seers, and novelists to see themselves as teachers. Whatever the social, psychological, political and economic basis for it in present-day Africa, this interchangeability of role between the creative writer and the prophet appears to be a specific phenomenon of underdevelopment and therefore, like it also, a passing or ephemeral phase.[9]

And he cites the authority of C. M. Bowra in support of his explanation. The fallacy of the argument lies, of course, in its assumption that when you talk about a people's "level of development" you define their total condition and assign them an indisputable and unambiguous place on mankind's evolutionary ladder; in other words, that you are enabled by the authority of that phrase to account for all their material as well as spiritual circumstance. Show me a people's plumbing, you say, and I can tell you their art.

I should have thought that the very example of the Hebrew poet/prophets which Dr. Anozie takes from Bowra to demonstrate underdevelopment and confusion of roles would have been enough to alert him to the folly of his thesis. Or is he seriously suggesting that the poetry of these men—Isaiah, for example—written, it seems, out of a confusion of roles, in an underdeveloped society, is less good than what is written today by poets who are careful to remain within the proper bounds of poetry within developed societies? Personally, I should be quite content to wallow in Isaiah's error and write "For unto us a child is born."

Incidentally, any reader who is at all familiar with some of the arguments that go on around modern African literature will have noticed that in the passage I have just quoted from Dr. Anozie he is not only talking about Okigbo but also alluding (with some disapproval) to a paper I read at Leeds University ten years ago which I called "The Novelist as

Teacher"; Anozie thus kills two weaverbirds dexterously with one stone! In his disapproval of what I had to say he follows, of course, in the footsteps of certain Western literary schoolmasters from whom I had already earned many sharp reprimands for that paper, who told me in clear terms that an artist had no business being so earnest.

It seems to me that this matter is of serious and fundamental importance, and must be looked at carefully. Earnestness and its opposite, levity, may be neither good nor bad in themselves but merely appropriate or inappropriate according to circumstance. I hold, however, and have held from the very moment I began to write, that earnestness *is* appropriate to my situation. Why? I suppose because I have a deep-seated need to alter things within that situation, to find for myself a little more room than has been allowed me in the world. I realize how pompous or even frightening this must sound to delicate sensibilities, but I can't help it.

The missionary who left the comforts of Europe to wander through my primeval forest was extremely earnest. He had to be; he came to change my world. The builders of empire who turned me into a "British protected person" knew the importance of being earnest; they had that quality of mind which Imperial Rome before them understood so well: *gravitas.* Now, it seems to me pretty obvious that if I desire to change the role and identity fashioned for me by those earnest agents of colonialism I will need to borrow some of their resolve. Certainly, I could not hope to do it through self-indulgent levity.

But of course I do appreciate also that the world is large and that all men cannot be, indeed must not be, of one mind. I appreciate that there are people in the world who have no need or desire to change anything. Perhaps they have already accomplished the right amount of change to ensure their own comfort. Perhaps they see the need for change but feel powerless to attempt it, or perhaps they feel it is someone else's business. For these people, earnestness is a dirty word or is simply tiresome. Even the evangelist, once so earnest and certain, now sits back in contemplation of his church, its foundation well and truly laid, its edifice rising majestically where once was jungle; the colonial governor who once brought his provinces so ruthlessly to heel prefers now to speak of the benefits of peace and orderly government. Certainly, they would much rather have easy-going natives under their jurisdiction than earnest ones—unless of course the earnestness be the perverse kind that turns in against itself.

The first nationalists and freedom fighters in the colonies, hardly concerned to oblige their imperial masters, were offensively earnest. They had no choice. They needed to alter the arrangement which kept them and their people out in the rain and the heat of the sun. They fought and won some victories. They changed a few things and seemed to secure certain powers of action over others. But quite quickly the great collusive swindle that was independence showed its true face to us. And we were dismayed; but only momentarily for even in our defeat we had gained something of inestimable value—a baptism of fire.

And so our world stands in just as much need of change today as it ever did in the past. Our writers responding to something in themselves and acting also within the traditional concept of an artist's role in society—using his art to control his environment—have addressed themselves to some of these matters in their art. And their concern seems to upset certain people whom history has dealt with differently and who persist in denying the validity of experiences and destinies other than theirs. And worst of all, some of our own critics who ought to guide these people out of their error seem so anxious to oblige them. Whatever the social, psychological, political and economic basis for this acquiescence, one hopes that it is only a passing and an ephemeral phase!

If this earnestness we speak of were manifested by just one or two writers in Africa there might perhaps be a good case for dismissing it out of hand. But look at the evidence:

Amos Tutuola has often given as a reason for his writing the need to preserve his traditional culture. It is true that a foreign critic, Adrian Roscoe, has chosen to jubilate over what appears to him like Tutuola's lack of "an awareness of cultural, national and racial affinities,"[10] but such an opinion may reflect more accurately his own wishful thinking than Tutuola's mind. Certainly a careful reading of *The Palm-Wine Drinkard* will not bear out the assertion that colonialism is "dead for him." Why would he go out of his way to tell us, for example, that "both white and black deads were living in the Dead's Town"[11] unless he considers the information significant, as indeed anyone who lived in the Lagos of the 1950s would readily appreciate? For although Nigeria experienced only "benign colonialism," it required a monumental demonstration of all nationalist organizations in the territory after a particularly blatant incident of racism in a Lagos hotel to compel the administration into token relaxation of the practice whereby Whites and Blacks lived in trim reservations or squalid townships separated by a regulation two-mile cordon sanitaire. Some day a serious critic interested in such matters will assemble and interpret Tutuola's many scattered allusions to colonialism for the benefit of more casual readers. For there are such intriguing incidents as the Drinkard's deliverance of the Red People from an ancient terror which required them to sacrifice one victim every year, for which blessing he lives among them for a while exploiting their cheap labour to develop and extend his plantations "becoming richer than the rest of the people in that town" until the moment of crisis arrives and he causes "the whole of them" to be wiped out. Such a critic will no doubt pay particular attention to the unperturbed and laconic comment of the deliverer's wife: ". . . all the lives of the natives were lost and the life of the non-natives saved."[12] But until that serious critic comes along, Mr. Roscoe can certainly have the comfort of believing that "if Achebe and Soyinka want to write in order to change the world, Tutuola has other reasons."

And then Camara Laye. As recently as 1972 he was saying in an interview:

> In showing the beauty of this culture, my novel testifies to its greatness. People who had not been aware that Africa had its own culture were able to grasp the significance of our past and our civilization. I believe that this understanding is the most meaningful contribution of African literature.[13]

The distinguished and versatile Sierra Leonian, Davidson Abioseh Nicol—scientist, writer and diplomat—explaining why he wrote, said:

> . . . because I found that most of those who wrote about us seldom gave any nobility to their African characters unless they were savages or servants or facing impending destruction. I knew differently.[14]

One could go on citing example after example of earnestness among African writers. But one final quotation—from

Kofi Awoonor, the fine Ghanaian poet, novelist and essayist
—should suffice:

> An African writer must be a person who has some kind of conception
> of the society in which he is living and the way he wants the society to
> go.[15]

All this juvenile earnestness must give unbearable offence
to mature people. Have we not heard, they may ask, what
Americans say—that the place for sending messages is the
Western Union? Perhaps we have; perhaps we haven't. But
the plain fact is that we are *not* Americans. Americans have
their vision; we have ours. We do not claim that ours is
superior; we only ask to keep it. For, as my forefathers said,
the firewood which a people have is adequate for the kind of
cooking they do. To levy a charge of underdevelopment
against African writers today may prove as misguided and
uninformed as a similar dismissal of African art by visitors of
an earlier age before the coming of Picasso. Those worthy
men saw little good around them, only child-like and grotesque distortions. Frank Willett, in his excellent book *African Art,* tells us of one such visitor to Benin in 1701, a certain
David Nyendael, who on being taken to the royal gallery
described the objects as being:

> . . . so wretchedly carved that it is hardly possible to distinguish
> whether they are most like men or beasts; notwithstanding which my
> guides were able to distinguish them into merchants, soldiers, wild
> beast hunters, etc.[16]

Most people today would be inclined to ascribe the
wretchedness to Nyendael's own mind and taste rather than
to the royal art of Benin. And yet, for me, his comment is
almost saved by his acknowledgement, albeit grudging, of

the very different perception of his guides, the real owners of the culture.

The colonialist critic, unwilling to accept the validity of sensibilities other than his own, has made particular point of dismissing the African novel. He has written lengthy articles to prove its non-existence largely on the grounds that the novel is a peculiarly Western genre, a fact which would interest us if our ambition was to write "Western" novels. But, in any case, did not the black people in America, deprived of their own musical instruments, take the trumpet and the trombone and blow them as they had never been blown before, as indeed they were not designed to be blown? And the result, was it not jazz? Is any one going to say that this was a loss to the world or that those first Negro slaves who began to play around with the discarded instruments of their masters should have played waltzes and foxtrots? No! Let every people bring their gifts to the great festival of the world's cultural harvest and mankind will be all the richer for the variety and distinctiveness of the offerings.

My people speak disapprovingly of an outsider whose wailing drowned the grief of the owners of the corpse. One last word to the owners. It is because our own critics have been somewhat hesitant in taking control of our literary criticism (sometimes—let's face it—for the good reason that we will not do the hard work that should equip us) that the task has fallen to others, some of whom (again we must admit) have been excellent and sensitive. And yet most of what remains to be done can best be tackled by ourselves, the owners. If we fall back, can we complain that others are rushing forward? A man who does not lick his lips, can he blame the harmattan for drying them?

Let us emulate those men of Benin, ready to guide the

curious visitor to the gallery of their art, willing to listen with politeness even to his hasty opinions but careful, most careful, to concede nothing to him that might appear to undermine their own position within their heritage or compromise the integrity of their indigenous perception. For supposing the artists of Benin and of Congo and Angola had agreed with Nyendael in 1701 and abandoned their vision and begun to make their images in the style of "developed" Portugal, would they not have committed a grave disservice to Africa and ultimately to Europe herself and the rest of the world? Because they did not, it so happened that after the passage of two centuries other Europeans, more sensitive by far than Nyendael, looked at their work again and learnt from it a new way to see the world.

8

Thoughts on the African Novel

MANY YEARS AGO at a writers' conference in Makerere, Uganda, I attempted (not very successfully) to get my colleagues to defer a definition of African literature which was causing us a lot of trouble. I suggested that the task might become easier when more of our produce had entered the market. That was ten years ago. I was saying in effect that African literature would define itself in action; so why not leave it alone? I still think it was excellent advice even if it carried a hint of evasiveness or even superstition.

I do admit to certain residual superstitions; and one of the

This address was published in the *Dalhousie Review,* vol. 53, no. 4, December 1973; subsequently in *Morning Yet on Creation Day,* Doubleday Anchor Books, 1975.

strongest is the fear of names, of hurrying to a conclusion
when the issue is still wide open. If I may paraphrase a
proverb which seems to me appropriate: Do not underrate a
day while an hour of light remains. In other words, be careful, for one hour is enough to do a man in.

> Edogo's mind was in pain over the child. Some people were already
> saying that perhaps he was none other than the first one. But Edogo
> and Amoge never talked about it; the woman especially was afraid.
> Since utterance had power to change fear into living truth they dared
> not speak before they had to.[1]

The world of the creative artist is like that. It is not the
world of the taxonomist whose first impulse on seeing a new
plant or animal is to define, classify and file away. Nor is it
the world of the taxidermist who plies an even less desirable
trade.

But I am never fully consistent, not even in my superstitions. I always find thoughts antagonistic to my secure position floating dangerously around it. It is these floating
thoughts I wish to talk to you about.

The first is that the African novel has to be about Africa.
A pretty severe restriction, I am told. But Africa is not only a
geographical expression; it is also a metaphysical landscape—
it is in fact a view of the world and of the whole cosmos
perceived from a particular position. This is as close to the
brink of chaos as I dare proceed. As for who an African
novelist is, it is partly a matter of passports, of individual
volition and particularly of seeing from that perspective I
have just touched with the timidity of a snail's horn. Being
an African, like being a Jew, carries certain penalties—as
well as benefits, of course. But perhaps more penalties than
benefits. Ben-Gurion once said: "If somebody wants to be a

Jew, that's enough for me." We could say the same for being an African. So it is futile to argue whether Conrad's *Heart of Darkness* is African literature. As far as I know, Joseph Conrad never even considered the possibility. In spite of all temptations he remained an Englishman! And it is not even a matter of colour. For we have Nadine Gordimer (who is here today), Doris Lessing and others.

And then language. As you know, there has been an impassioned controversy about an African literature in non-African languages. But what is a *non-African* language? English and French certainly. But what about Arabic? What about Swahili even? Is it then a question of how long the language has been present on African soil? If so, how many years should constitute *effective occupation?* For me it is again a pragmatic matter. A language spoken by Africans on African soil, a language in which Africans write, justifies itself.

I fully realize that I am beginning to sound like a bad dictionary—the type you take a strange word to and it defines it with a stranger word; you look *that* up and it gives you back your original strange word; so you end up with two mysteries instead of one! But that is the reality of our situation, and it is surely more useful to begin to deal with its complexity than to propose catchy but impossible simplifications.

At the root of all these strange and untidy thoughts lies a monumental historical fact, Europe—a presence which has obsessed us from Equiano to Ekwensi. For Equiano a preoccupation with Europe was pretty inevitable. After all, he had only just recently freed himself from actual enslavement to Europeans. He lived in Europe and was married to a European. His ancestral Igboland had become a fragmented memory.

In our own time a preoccupation with Europe has seemed almost equally inevitable despite the passage of nearly two hundred years. In the colonial period and its aftermath we were preoccupied with Europe in the form of protest. Then a bunch of bright ones came along and said: "We are through with intoning the colonial litany. We hereby repudiate the crippling legacy of a Europe-oriented protest. We are tough-minded. We absolve Europe of all guilt. Don't you worry, Europe, we were bound to violence long before you came to our shores." Naturally, Europe, which was beginning to believe the worst about itself, is greatly relieved and impressed by the mental emancipation, objectivity and sophistication of these newcomers. As if any intelligent writer of protest had ever taken a starry-eyed view of Africa or doubted the reality of evil in Africa, the new anti-protest, broad-minded writer will now endorse the racist theory that Africa *is* evil, *is* the heart of darkness.

It is this illusion of objectivity, this grotesque considerateness, this perverse charitableness which asks a man to cut his own throat for the comfort and good opinion of another, that I must now address myself to.

Quite often the malady (for it is indeed a sickness) shows fairly mild symptoms and is widespread; at other times it comes in its virulent forms. But mild or severe, it manifests itself as self-disgust and an obscene eagerness to please our adversary.

There is a Nigerian academic who went to study in Britain in the late 1920s and decided to become an Englishman. So he settled down in Britain after his studies, married and raised a family, and by all accounts was a perfectly happy man. Forty years later as a result of an unhappy conjunction of events he found himself appointed to an administrative position in a Nigerian university. To his first press interviewer he boasted that he spoke no Nigerian language. He cannot recognize Nigerian food, let alone eat it. Given a chance he will appoint a European over a Nigerian to teach at his university; his argument: a university, as the name implies, is a universal institution.

But fortunately, this man is not a writer. For wouldn't it be awful if writers—those bright hopes of our society—should become afflicted with such a warped vision; a vision which creates a false polarity between an object and its abstraction and places its focus on the abstraction? Personally, I am no longer entirely optimistic. Let me present two short passages of the kind that has been causing me great discomfort:

> This is the confrontation which *The Interpreters* presents. It is not an "African" problem. Events all over the world have shown in the new generation a similar dissatisfaction . . . Thus Soyinka, using a Nigerian setting, has portrayed a universal problem. This is what makes both this novel and the whole corpus of Soyinka's work universally valid.[2]

Before I go on, let me make two points. First, I am not concerned with Professor Eldred Jones's evaluation of Soyinka but with the terms he has chosen for that evaluation. The second point is that I regard Eldred Jones as our finest literary scholar, a man of great sensitivity and perception whom I should have much preferred not to disagree with. But the dogma of universality which he presents here (I believe, absent-mindedly) is so patently false and dangerous and yet so attractive that it ought not to go unchallenged. For

supposing "events all over the world" have *not* shown "in
the new generation a similar dissatisfaction . . . ," would it
truly be invalid for a Nigerian writer seeing a dissatisfaction
in *his* society to write about it? Am I being told, for Christ's
sake, that before I write about any problem I must first verify
whether they have it too in New York and London and
Paris?

What Professor Eldred Jones is proposing is that I re-
nounce my vision, which (since I do not work with the radio
telescope at Jodrell Bank) is necessarily local and particular.
Not so long ago a similar proposition was made to me, an
attempt to discredit my vision and the absolute validity of my
experience. But it came from "expected quarters." At the end
of the war in Nigeria (in which, you may know, I was on the
wrong side), I had an invitation to visit New Guinea and
Australia. But some official or officials in Lagos saw to it that
I did not get a passport. When I protested to the Commissioner for External Affairs he wrote me a nice, intriguing
letter with words to this effect:

Dear Achebe,
Thank you for your letter in which you complained about difficulties
which you thought you had with my officials . . .

You can see, can't you, the close kinship between that
letter and the proposition by Eldred Jones? They are both
telling me to be careful in defining "difficulties." Because
other people may not agree, I had better check my vision
with them before saying what I see. Such a proposition is
dangerous and totally unacceptable, for once you agree to
"clear" your vision with other people you are truly in trouble.

Now let us look at another short extract from the same

essay by Eldred Jones quoted in *Introduction to Nigerian Literature*:

> When Wole Soyinka writes like this his audience is not a local one; it is a universal one. Indeed at this point he widens his immediate range of reference by making the Court Historian invoke the precedent of the Trojan War.[3]

Thus, in the first extract Eldred Jones praises Wole Soyinka for not writing about an African problem but a universal one; and in the second for not writing for a local but a universal audience! Surely, African criticism must be the only one in the whole world (or perhaps universe) where literary merit is predicated on such outlandish criteria. But as I said earlier I don't really believe that Eldred Jones thought seriously about this. He has simply and uncritically accepted the norms of some of the prevailing colonialist criticism, which I must say is most unlike him. Perhaps I should point out in fairness also that in the first extract he did put "African" in quotes, although it is not clear to me what exactly the quotes are supposed to do. Perhaps they hint at a distinction between *real* and *so-called* African problems. This may redeem the situation somewhat, but not very much. For *real* and *so-called* Africa can and do become metaphysical retreats for all kinds of prejudice. Thus a certain critic many years ago said of Ekwensi's *Burning Grass:* "At last Ekwensi has drawn real Nigerian characters . . ." without saying what unreal Nigerian characters looked like. But one sensed that a Lagosian or an African from Nairobi might be deemed less real than a Masai or a Tuareg; surely a matter of social taste and not of literary criticism!

I shall look at one other aspect of the same problem and I shall be done. In our discussion yesterday, Professor Emile

Snyder reminded us that politics was always present in literature and gave examples ranging from Dante to Eliot. Why, he asked, do we get so worked up about it in discussing African literature? Of course the reason is that we are late starters. I mean really late—after the prizes are all given out and the track judges have packed up their things and gone home. Such late starters are generally very conscientious. Though no one is looking, they will cut no corners.

That is why, for instance, we must now have our own debate on art for art's sake. Why we must have pundits decreeing to us what is or is not appropriate to literature; what genres are for us and what we may only touch at our peril. Why literary legislators pass laws telling us what social and political roles artists may (but more usually, may not) perform.

Thus, in a curious novel entitled *The Trial of Christopher Okigbo,* Ali Mazrui has a poet tried in the hereafter for throwing away his life on the battlefield like any common tribesman. There is no condemnation of war as such, only of poets getting involved—for "some lives are more sacred than others." In the words of one of the novel's leading characters (an African Perry Mason clearly admired by Mazrui): ". . . a great artist was first of all an individualist, secondly a universalist, and only thirdly a social collectivist." Since these roles and attributes are not known instinctively by the artist in question (otherwise how would Okigbo not know what was legitimate activity for him?), it stands to reason that he requires someone like Mazrui to tell him (a) the precise moment when he crosses the threshold of mere artist and becomes a great artist and (b) how to juggle with his three marbles of individualism, universalism and social collectivism.

What I am saying really boils down to a simple plea for the African novel. Don't fence me in.

I dare not close without a word of recognition for that small and proprietary school of critics who assure us that the African novel does not exist. Reason: the novel was invented in England. For the same kind of reason I shouldn't know how to drive a car because I am no descendant of Henry Ford. But every visitor to Nigeria will tell you that we are among the world's most creative drivers!

In conclusion, all these prescriptions and proscriptions, all these dogmas about the universal and the eternal verities; all this proselytizing for European literary fashions, even dead ones; all this hankering after definitions may in the end prove worse than futile by creating needless anxieties. For as everybody knows, anxiety can hinder creative performance, from sex to science.

I have no doubt at all about the existence of the African novel. This form of fiction has seized the imagination of many African writers and they will use it according to their differing abilities, sensibilities and visions without seeking anyone's permission. I believe it will grow and prosper. I believe it has a great future.

Recently one of my students pointed to a phrase on the cover of Camara Laye's *The Radiance of the King* and said, "Do you agree with that?" It was a comment credited to my good friend Ezekiel Mphahlele, to the effect that this was "the great African novel." I told the student that I had nothing to say because I had an interest in the matter; and I'm glad to say, the joke was well taken. Actually, I admire *The Radiance of the King* quite a lot; still, I do hope that the great African novel will not be about a disreputable European.

Halifax, Canada, 1973

9

 Work and Play

in Tutuola's

 The Palm-Wine Drinkard

A YOUNG NIGERIAN WOMAN doing a higher de-
gree in America said to me when I taught there in the 1970s,
"I hear you teach Tutuola." It was not a simple statement;
her accent was heavy with accusation. We discussed the matter for a while and it became quite clear that she considered
The Palm-Wine Drinkard to be childish and crude and certainly not the kind of thing a patriotic Nigerian should be
exporting to America. Back in Nigeria a few years later I also
noticed a certain condescension among my students towards
the book and a clear indication that they did not consider it
good enough to engage the serious attention of educated
adults like themselves. They could not see what it was about.

The first Equiano Memorial Lecture, University of Ibadan, 15 July 1977.

Now, if I were one of those who hold the view that literature does not have to be about anything I would have been able to tell that young woman and those students of mine not to worry—that "this tall devilish story" (as Dylan Thomas called it) should be enjoyed solely for its own sake, as "literature in the service of itself," as the work of "a writer without problems."[1]

"Problems" in this context, we must understand, is the apparently misguided and old-fashioned desire on the part of some African writers to prove a point or teach a moral in their writing which some advanced critics tell us is so unworthy! Actually, Tutuola does have "problems"; he is the most moralistic of all Nigerian writers, being fully as single-minded in the matter as the chap-book authors of the Onitsha Market. His superiority over those pamphlet writers has nothing to do with a vision of "literature in the service of itself," but arises out of a richer imagination and a more soundly based moralism. For while they are offering a half-baked ethic of escapism from the pressures of modern township living, he has his two feet firmly planted in the hard soil of an ancient oral, and moral, tradition.

Of course, Tutuola's art conceals—or rather clothes—his purpose, as all good art must do. But anybody who asks what the story is about can hardly have read him. And I suspect that many who talk about Tutuola one way or another are yet to read him.

The first two sentences in *The Palm-Wine Drinkard* tell us clearly enough what the story is about:

> I was a palm-wine drinkard since I was a boy of ten years of age. I had no other work more than to drink palm-wine in my life.[2]

The reader may, of course, be so taken with Tutuola's vigorous and unusual prose style or beguiled by that felicitous coinage, "drinkard," that he misses the social and ethical question being proposed: What happens when a man immerses himself in pleasure to the exclusion of all work; when he raises pleasure to the status of work and occupation and says in effect: "Pleasure be thou my work!"? *The Palm-Wine Drinkard* is a rich and spectacular exploration of this gross perversion, its expiation through appropriate punishment and the offender's final restoration. That's what the story is about.

Tutuola does not waste any time exploring or elaborating on the offence itself. The offender/protagonist/narrator states the case simply and bluntly in those two short sentences on page one, gives an equally brief and precise background to it, and proceeds to spend the rest of the book on the punishment he undergoes in atonement for his offence and then a fairly brief coda on his restoration.

This disposition of emphases might appear somewhat uneven to the "modern" reader brought up on lengthy psychological interpretations of guilt. But Tutuola belongs primarily to humanity's earlier tradition which could say simply: "Thou shalt not commit murder," without necessarily having to explore what motivations might lurk in murky prenatal experience! But he also knows perhaps instinctively what the moderns are all about and so makes a gesture to them in this seemingly harmless piece of family background:

> But when my father noticed that I could not do any work more than to drink, he engaged an expert palm-wine tapster for me; he had no other work more than to tap palm-wine every day.[3]

Again, Tutuola has packed into a simple and brief statement a huge social and ethical proposition: A man who will not work can only stay alive if he can somehow commandeer to his own use the labour of other people either by becoming a common thief or a slave-owner. Thanks to the affluence of a father (he "was the richest man in our town"), who is willing to indulge his son's outrageous appetite, the Drinkard is enabled to buy a slave and to press him into a daily round of exploitative and socially useless work. The point is therefore made quite clearly—lest we be tempted to dismiss the Drinkard's love of palm-wine as a personal drinking problem—that refusal to work cannot be a simple "self-regarding act" but is a social and moral offence of colossal consequence.

Tutuola's moral universe is one in which work and play in their numerous variations complement each other. The good life, he seems to say, is that in which business and pleasure, striving and repose, giving and receiving, suffering and enjoyment, punishment and reprieve, poverty and wealth, have their place, their time and their measure. We *give* work and struggle; and in the end we *take* rest and fulfilment.

Nothing in all this is particularly original. What is so very impressive is Tutuola's inventiveness in creating new and unexpected circumstances for the unfolding of the theme. For example, to make the point that those whose personal circumstance shields them from the necessity to work are really unfortunate and deprived and must do something to remedy their lack, Tutuola creates the rather dramatic and mysterious, and in the end quite terrible, personage, the Invisible Pawn, otherwise known as Give and Take, who comes to the Drinkard out of the night and tells how he has always heard the word "poor" without really knowing it and asks for help in order to make its acquaintance. Simbi, a character in

Tutuola's later book, has, like the Drinkard, a much too easy childhood and deals with it herself by going out in search of hardship. The Drinkard has too much appetite and too little wisdom to recognize his predicament unaided and has to be forced into dealing with it. I think that one should make the point here that Tutuola's conception of poverty as creative experience is very different from the view which gave rise in the past to the profession of poverty in certain religions or in societies where the poor are encouraged to make a living out of the mendicant's bowl. I suspect that Tutuola would consider these manifestations as gross and mistaken. For he is concerned not with poverty as an alternative way of life nor with affluence as necessarily evil. The creative potential of poverty in his vision is really no more than its ability to expose to the world of work those who might otherwise escape its rigours. The romantic fad of patched and dirty jeans among the young of affluent societies today which fakes poverty rather painlessly would not seem to fall into Tutuola's scheme either.

Even a moderately careful reading of *The Palm-Wine Drinkard* reveals a number of instances where Tutuola, by consistently placing work and play in close sequence, appears quite clearly to be making a point.

In the episode of the Three Good Creatures we see how music relieves the Drinkard and his wife of the curse of their half-bodied baby. They have just danced non-stop for five days and find themselves unexpectedly rid of their intolerable burden. But right away they also realise that after the dance the life of struggle must be resumed and its details attended to:

> Then after we had left these creatures and our half-bodied baby, we
> started a fresh journey . . . But we were penniless . . . then I
> thought within myself how could we get money for our food etc.[4]

And so the poet/drinkard who has just sung a lofty pane-
gyric to the three personifications of music, and danced for
five days without pausing even to eat, now suddenly becomes
a practical man again concerned with money and "food etc."
He carves a paddle, turns himself into a canoe and his wife
into a boatman. At the end of the first day they have garnered seven pounds, five shillings and three pence from ferry-
ing passengers across the river. (One small point here: the
reformed, or rather reforming, Drinkard is a magician and
from time to time does exploit his supernatural powers, but
he always has to combine this ability with honest-to-God
work. So although he can turn himself into a canoe, he still
needs to carve a real paddle!)

If this episode were the only instance in the book where
Tutuola makes the point of restoring the ascendancy of work
after a binge, one would probably not be justified in attach-
ing particular significance to it, striking though it certainly is.
But we do find Tutuola returning again and again to the
same motif. In fact, later in the book there is another "special
occasion" involving Drum, Dance and Song again. This time
the merriment is to celebrate the deliverance of the Red People from an ancient curse and the founding of their new city.
On this occasion even Drum, Dance and Song surpass themselves. Such is the power of their music that "people who had
been dead for hundreds of years rose up and came to witness":

> The whole people of the new town, the whole people that rose up
> from the grave, animals, snakes, Spirits and other nameless crea-
> tures . . .[5]

join in the merriment. The cosmic upheaval unleashed by the
three primogenitors of music is only quelled and natural
order restored after they have been banished permanently
from the world so that only the memory of their visit remains
with mankind. Quite clearly the primal force of their presence has proved too strong for the maintenance of the
world's work. Immediately after their gigantic display and
banishment Tutuola switches abruptly and dramatically to
the theme of work to clinch the point:

> So when these three fellows (Drum, Song and Dance) disappeared,
> the people of the new town went back to their houses . . . After I
> had spent a year with my wife in this new town, I became a rich man.
> Then I hired many labourers to clear bush for me and it was cleared
> up to three miles square . . . then I planted the seeds and grain.[6]

One could give other examples of Tutuola's juxtaposition
of work and play in *The Palm-Wine Drinkard*. Indeed, it
becomes possible, I believe, to see the proper balance between
them as a fundamental law of Tutuola's world, and the consequences of its infringement as the central meaning of the
book.

In addition to the primary balance between work and play
in the grand design of *The Palm-Wine Drinkard* we notice
also a subordinate or secondary system of interior balance
between particularly harsh sectors of the Drinkard's ordeal
and recuperative periods of rest. Compared to the sectors of
hardship the periods of respite are few and brief—suggesting
a deficit of rest which is however fully justified by the
Drinkard's previous life of indolent frivolity. But though

brief and sporadic these intervening episodes of rest/play manage to stand out in arresting prominence, as in the episodes of the White Tree, Wraith Island and Wrong Town. Of these the White Tree yields the richest harvest of interpretation and I should like to examine it a little closely.

The episode of the White Tree occurs immediately after the Drinkard and his wife have endured at the hands of the sadistic inhabitants of Unreturnable-heaven's Town the most savage torture of the entire journey. It thus seems quite appropriate that after such suffering the travellers should now enjoy their most elaborate rest. But the ease and luxury they do encounter in the White Tree surpass all expectations. Free food and drink in a cabaret atmosphere and a gambling casino are among the amenities of this European-style haven of conspicuous consumption. Predictably the Drinkard very quickly relapses into his old addictions:

> I began to lavish all the drinks as I had been a great palm-wine drinkard in my town before I left.[7]

And naturally also he loses the will for the quest, so that when Faithful Mother tells him that it is time to resume his journey, he begs to be permitted to stay in the Tree for ever. When she tells him that this is impossible, he makes a second plea—for her to accompany them to the end of the journey. Again she says no. Totally disconsolate the Drinkard then contemplates a third possibility: death. But even that escape is also impossible for him or his wife because they have already sold their death.

I think that what Tutuola is saying here is very important for an understanding of the meaning of the story. The three ways in which the pilgrim might seek to evade the rigours of a dangerous quest are taken up in turn and rejected: he may not prolong the interlude of rest and enjoyment at the inn; he may not be assisted to arrive at his destination without the trouble of travelling; he may not opt out of the struggle through premature death.

As the Drinkard and his wife resume their journey there is even an oblique suggestion that their recent interlude in the White Tree has been of the insubstantial nature of a dream:

> . . . it was just as if a person slept in his or her room, but when he woke up, he found himself or herself inside a big bush.[8]

If we accept this suggestion the implication may well be that play, though a necessary restorative, is not only a temporary but even an illusory escape from the reality of waking life, which is work with its attendant pain and suffering.

The Drinkard's fault, as we said earlier, is that he attempted to subvert the order of things and put play in the place of work. He does this because he has an appetite which knows no limit or boundary. His punishment is exact and appropriate. He is launched on a quest in which he is obliged to wage adequate struggle to compensate for his previous idleness. While he is undergoing this learning process he is shown many positive examples from other people of what his own life should have been. We have already referred to the visit made to him one night by Give and Take. Then there is the example of Death himself at work in his garden; and there is the king of Wraith Island, who neglects to invite the smallest creature in his kingdom to join in communal work and is compelled to offer apologies to the little fellow for the slight.

But perhaps the most striking object lesson for the Drinkard is the terrible son born from his wife's swollen thumb. Although the Drinkard may not know or acknowledge it, this child is like a distorting mirror reflecting his father's image in even less flattering proportions. He is really Palm-Wine Drinkard Junior, in other words. He has the same insatiable appetite, the same lack of self-control and moderation, the same readiness to victimize and enslave others. He is of course an altogether nastier person than his father, but the essential ingredients of character are the same.

There is a secondary theme which runs beside that of work and play and finally meets and merges with it. This is what I shall call the theme of boundaries. A few incidents in the novel will elucidate this.

As the Drinkard and his wife leave Wraith Island we see the friendly inhabitants come out and accompany them to the frontier, and then stop. And we are told quite explicitly by the Drinkard that

> . . . if it was in their power they would have led us to our destination, but they were forbidden to touch another creature's land or bush.[9]

Similarly, at the end of the sojourn in the White Tree the travellers, disinclined, as we have seen, to resume their arduous quest, ask Faithful Mother to lead them to the end of the journey: "But she told us that she could not do such a request because she must not go beyond their boundary."[10]

There are numerous other instances in the book where boundaries play a decisive role in the plot. For instance, a monster may be pursuing the travellers furiously and then suddenly and unexpectedly stop at some frontier such as a road. And we have a variant of the same basic prohibition in the case of Give and Take, who "could not do anything in the day time"—thus observing a boundary erected in time rather than space. And finally the Drinkard is to learn on setting foot at last on Dead's Town that "it was forbidden for alives to come to the Dead's Town"[11]—an example of what we might perhaps call an existential boundary!

What all this means is that here in this most unlikely of places, this jungle where everything seems possible and lawlessness might have seemed quite natural, there is yet a law of jurisdiction which sets a limit to the activity of even the most unpredictable of its rampaging demons. Because no monster however powerful is allowed a free run of the place, anarchy is held—precariously, but held—at bay, so that a traveller who perseveres can progress from one completed task to the domain of another and in the end achieve progressively the creative, moral purpose in the extraordinary but by no means arbitrary universe of Tutuola's story.

This law of boundaries operates more subtly but no less powerfully at other levels in *The Palm-Wine Drinkard.* A boundary implies a duality of jurisdictions both of which must be honoured if there is to be order in the world. Tutuola suggests that promise and fulfilment constitute one such duality, for a promise is no less than a pledge for future work, a solemn undertaking to work later if you can play now. Consequently, we find that Tutuola never allows a broken promise to go unpunished. There are quite a few examples of such breach and punishment in the book but we shall only refer to the case of the Drinkard's father-in-law. We may recall that this man has promised that if the Drinkard rescues his daughter he will direct him towards the goal of his quest. The Drinkard performs his part of the bargain, but the man, not wishing to part from his daughter, who has in the meantime married the Drinkard, begins to prevaricate. Consequently, the Drinkard tarries in his father-in-law's town for three years. It is during this time that a terrible scourge of a child is born to the young couple, a child who begins straight away to terrorize the town. He causes so much havoc that the community conspire to burn him to ashes. After this experience the old man needs no further persuasion to give his son-in-law the information he has withheld for years in breach of his promise.

The principle of unfulfilled promise explored in this episode and elsewhere is developed further and given a new twist in the activities of that strange personage called Give and Take. You will recall that when we first encounter him he is meekly seeking to enlarge his experience by knowing poverty at first hand. The Drinkard obliges him by setting him up to taste the bitter life of an indentured labourer. Later, we learn to our great surprise that Give and Take is no ordinary fellow but "the head of all the Bush-creatures . . . and the most powerful in the world of the Bush-creatures." This mysterious monarch of the jungle does get the experience he seeks but in the process establishes the principle behind his name: that a community which lets some invisible hand do its work for it will sooner or later forfeit the harvest. Give and Take proves a merciless exactor; for the labour he has given he takes not only the people's crops but, in the conflict that ensues, their lives as well.

Finally, we can also apply the concept of boundaries to the dual jurisdictions of work and play. Because the Drinkard's appetite knows no limit or boundary, he takes and takes without giving and allows play not just to transgress but wholly and totally to overrun the territory of work. His ordeal in the jungle of correction changes him from a social parasite to a leader and a teacher whose abiding gift to his people is to create the condition in which they can overcome want and reliance on magic, and return to the arts of agriculture and husbandry.

"Relevance" is a word bandied around very much in contemporary expression, but it still has validity nonetheless. In *The Palm-Wine Drinkard,* Tutuola is weaving more than a tall, devilish story. He is speaking strongly and directly to our times. For what could be more relevant than a celebration of work today for the benefit of a generation and a people whose heroes are no longer makers of things and ideas but spectacular and insatiable consumers?

10

Don't Let Him Die:
A Tribute
to Christopher Okigbo

CHRISTOPHER OKIGBO could not enter or leave a room unremarked; yet he was not extravagant in manner or appearance. There was something about him not easy to define, a certain inevitability of drama and event. His vibrancy and heightened sense of life touched everyone he came into contact with. It is not surprising therefore that the young poet/artist Kevin Echeruo, who died even younger, soon after Okigbo, should have celebrated him as *ogbanje,* one of those mysterious, elusive and often highly talented beings who hurry to leave the world and to come again; or that Pol Ndu, who was to die in a road disaster, every gory detail of

Preface to *Don't Let Him Die,* eds. Chinua Achebe and Dubem Okafor, Fourth Dimension Publishing Company, Enugu, 1978.

which he had predicted in a poem five years earlier, should call Okigbo a seer.

Okigbo's exit was, for me, totally in character. I can see him clearly in his white "gown" and cream trousers among the vast crowd milling around my bombed apartment, the first spectacle of its kind in the Biafran capital in the second month of the war. I doubt that we exchanged more than a sentence or two. There were scores of sympathizers pressing forward to commiserate with me or praise God that my life and the lives of my wife and children had been spared. So I hardly caught more than a glimpse of him in that crowd and then he was gone like a meteor, forever.

That elusive impression is the one that lingers out of so many. As a matter of fact, he and I had talked for two solid hours that very morning. But in retrospect, that earlier meeting seems to belong to another time.

He had suddenly appeared at Citadel Press, the little publishing house we had set up together in the safe stronghold of Enugu after our flight—he from Ibadan and I from Lagos. He came like that from the war a few times to discuss our publishing programme. That morning our editorial chat had been interrupted by the sudden drone of an enemy aircraft overhead and the hectic and ineffectual small-arms fire that was supposed to scare it away, rather like a lot of flies worrying a bull. Not a very powerful bull, admittedly, at that point in the conflict before the Russians beat the British to it and supplied jet fighters to the Federal Army. In fact, air raids then were crude jokes that could almost be laughed off. People used to say that the safest thing was to go out into the open and keep an eye on the bomb as it was pushed out of the invading propeller aircraft! As Christopher and I listened uneasily, an explosion went off in the distance somewhere and the attack was soon over. We completed our discussion and parted. But that explosion which sounded so distant from the Citadel offices was to bring him back for a final silent farewell on that eventful day.

When he took the decision to join the army he went to great lengths to conceal his intention from me for fear, no doubt, that I might attempt to dissuade him from taking that hazardous step. I probably would have tried. He made up an elaborate story about an imminent and secret mission he was asked to undertake to Europe which put me totally off the scent. But to make absolutely certain, he borrowed my travelling bag and left his brown briefcase with me. When I saw him again two weeks later he was a major by special commission in the Biafran Army, though I never saw him in uniform. He always came to Citadel Press in civilian clothes.

One afternoon I was driving from Enugu to my village, Ogidi, where I lived following the bombing. My car radio was tuned to Lagos. Like all people caught in the mesh of modern war we soon became radio addicts. We wanted to hear the latest from the fronts; we wanted to hear what victories Nigeria was claiming next, not just from NBC Lagos, but even more extravagantly from Radio Kaduna. We needed to hear what the wider world had to say to all that—the BBC, the Voice of America, the French Radio, Cameroon Radio, Radio Ghana, Radio Anywhere. The Biafran forces had just suffered a major setback in the northern sector of the war by the loss of the university town of Nsukka. They had suffered an even greater morale-shattering blow in the death of that daring and enigmatic hero who had risen from military anonymity to legendary heights in the short space of eighteen months, Major Chukwuma Kaduna Nzeogwu, the leader of the first military coup in Nigeria. Before his enlist-

ment, Okigbo had begun to talk more and more about Nzeogwu, but I had not listened very closely; the military didn't
fascinate me as it did him. Driving almost mechanically in an
open stretch of roadway I was only half-listening to the radio
when suddenly Christopher Okigbo's name stabbed my slack
consciousness into panic life. Rebel troops wiped out by gal-
lant Federal forces. Among rebel officers killed: Major Christopher Okigbo.

I pulled up at the roadside. The open parkland around
Nachi stretched away in all directions. Other cars came and
passed. Had no one else heard the terrible news? When I
finally got myself home and told my family, my three-year-
old son screamed: "Daddy, don't let him die!" He and Christopher had been special pals. Whenever Chris had come to
the house the boy would climb on his knees, seize hold of his
fingers and strive with all his power to break them while
Christopher would moan in pretended agony. "Children are
wicked little devils," he would say to my wife and me over
the little fellow's head and let out more cries of pain. Christopher (he always preferred the full name to Chris) had a
gift for fellowship surpassing anything I had ever seen or
thought possible. He had friends, admirers, fans, cronies of
both sexes, from all ages, all social classes, all professions, all
ethnic groups, in Nigeria and everywhere. He was greedy for
friendship as indeed he was for all experience, for risk and
danger. He never took anti-malaria drugs because he rather
enjoyed the cosy, delirious fever he had when malaria got
him down about once a year. He relished challenges and the
more unusual or difficult, the better it made him feel. He
went to Government College, Umuahia, which did not teach
Latin, and yet opted for classics at the university. After grad-
uation he rapidly ran up a list of jobs that reads like a manual

of careers: civil servant, business man, teacher, librarian, publisher, industrialist, soldier. A mutual friend who is a professional librarian was somewhat scandalized when Okigbo announced that he was going to Nsukka to be interviewed for a position in the library of the new university. Reminded that he knew nothing about librarianship, Okigbo blithely replied that he had bought a book on the subject and intended to read it during the 400-mile journey to the interview. And he got the job!

Although he turned his hand to many things in his short life he never did anything badly or half-heartedly. He carried into all his performance a certain inborn finesse and a sense of elegance. When he fell in August 1967 in Ekwegbe, close to Nsukka where his poetry had come to sudden flower seven short years earlier, news of his death sent ripples of shock in all directions. Given the man and the circumstance it was impossible for everyone to react to the terrible loss in the same way. The varied responses, I think, would have pleased Okigbo enormously, for as he once said he liked to get to London a different way each time—sometimes via Rome, sometimes Barcelona and sometimes direct.

When his nephew, Dubem Okafor, and I put together a collection of poems in memory of him in 1978, the variety of the tributes bore witness to the power of the man's personality, his poetry, his life and death. Some of the contributors were close friends of his; some only knew him slightly, and others not at all. Some were his fellow countrymen, sundered at the time of his death by a horrendous fratricidal conflict and today still made uneasy by its memory, repercussions and the hypocrisy it engendered. Some were fellow Africans who may have heard Okigbo declare at Makerere in one of his impish moods that he wrote his poetry only for poets; and some from far-away West Indies, U.S.A., Canada and Great Britain. Some of the poems were written within a few weeks of his death and some several years later. And to underline further the variety of the Okigbo phenomenon, two poems in Igbo were included.

However intriguing his life or rich our memory of him as man, colleague and friend, it is primarily his poetry that commands this tribute. He was not only the finest Nigerian poet of his generation but I believe that as his work becomes better and more widely known in the world he will also be recognized as one of the most remarkable anywhere in our time. In Nigeria and in Africa a growing body of poets too young to have known him are under his spell; twenty years after his death he is the most widely imitated African poet.

His best poetry is more appealing and rewarding with every reading, always starting new ripples of significance. Critics have often charged him with obscurity. "Occasional inaccessibility" would be a more accurate phrase, for even at his most arcane moments there is never a blocking of vision in his poetry as there often is in some of his contemporaries. He always remains as visually clear as fine crystal glass. Barring a few obvious mystifications in his early work which he deleted from later editions, the "obscurity" in his poetry comes from a "straining among the echoes" to deliver his own authentic lines.

There is nothing in Nigerian poetry and little in any poetry I know to surpass the haunting beauty, the mystic resonance and clarity of the final movements of the protagonist's quest in "Distances." And the reader who cares to look will see in all its detail the spiritual landscape in which the prodigal, weary of travel, is called at last by the goddess into her cavern. The geometric shapes of his final passageway and the strange phosphorescent inscriptions they bear are all un-forgettably portrayed.

Okigbo was killed twenty years ago. But he had taken good care to ensure that he will not die.

11

Kofi Awoonor as a Novelist

KOFI AWOONOR is better known for his poetry—a strong, controlled poetry—that manages the miracle of muscular power and delicate accents of song, much of it inspired by the oral performances of his Ewe homeland in Ghana. He has also written some of the most thoughtful scholarly criticism of African life and letters.

In 1971 he made his novelistic début with *This Earth, My Brother* . . . , which he called "an allegorical tale of Africa."

An allegory is as good a name as one can call this rather unusual and highly personal form. It is in fact a medley of

Introduction to Doubleday/Anchor edition of *This Earth, My Brother* . . . , 1971.

forms—intense and tight sequences of poetic prose alternating with more open stretches of realistic narrative and now and again broken by shots of running commentary, all moving sometimes forward in time, sometimes backward or in circles, and at yet other times completely flung outside our accustomed historical time scale.

And yet we are never left behind but swept along the open highways of this eccentric journey or squeezed through its narrow twists, feeling no fatigue whatever (like the demented hero in his last long trek), yet tasting all the pain of the way to the cumulative disaster of its end which, strangely, was always there, around the corner even from the beginning; it is that death which we are told by the hero is always "hiding behind [a man's] door."

The story is an allegory of contemporary Africa:

> . . . a land of laughing people, very hospitable people. That's what the tourist posters proclaim. They forgot to add that pussy is cheap here, the liquor is indifferent, and the people suffer from a thousand diseases, there are beggars on the tarmac at the airport, and the leaders of government, any government, are amenable to fine financial pressures of undetermined favors.
>
> Lionel was talking about riding the first tank into Johannesburg when the revolution comes. My head erect like that of Conrad's Nigger of the Narcissus, I walk the noon through Covent Garden in search of the theatre where Niggers Everywhere Arise is playing, I carry my repulsive mask of a nigger's soul into a pub on Tottenham Court Road with Roger: when I snapped my fingers in remembrance of what I wanted to say, the publican with yellow teeth barked I am not a dog. No sir, you are not a dog. I am. The dog that died.
>
> Swinging, our nation's pentagon smashes the bludgeoned heads of orphans for a balancing trick of stability.

So despite those laughing people, laughing with all their white teeth, Africa is a place of torment and ugliness. Being Ghanaian, and Ghana being so central to modern Africa, Awoonor can sometimes particularize his Africa into his Ghana—a "revolting malevolence" he calls it, reminding us of that other Ghanaian writer, Ayi Kwei Armah, author of the novel *The Beautyful Ones Are Not Yet Born.*

Awoonor's allegory teems with people, places, incidents, thoughts, emotions, actions, evasions. It follows (pursues may be more apt) the hero from the very orgasm of his conception through his feverish life. It takes off without warning to any part of the world and makes unscheduled stops where it pleases. Yet despite such wide ranging techniques Awoonor never falls into preciousness or superficialities. What he unfolds before us may be fleeting but it is always sharp and never, one is convinced, unimportant. And it is not a succession of haphazard impressions either, despite the seeming arbitrariness of its sequences. There is a cumulativeness, indeed an organic, albeit bizarre, development towards the ultimate failure. But here is no existential futility; at every stage there is a misty hint of a viable alternative, of a road that is not taken, of a possibility that fails to develop. The central failure is African independence, whose early promise is like the butterfly that the child Amamu caught in the fields of yellow sunflowers wide as the moon, and it flew away again. He searched for it for days and found others that looked like it; but no, it was gone. Or his childhood love to the shadowy cousin who died at twelve of a mysterious pain that chewed her intestines, a love he was to spend his life searching for and not finding—certainly not from his been-to wife, Alice, nor even from his more understanding mistress, though she tried harder.

African independence ought to have succeeded, coming as it did at the end of a subjection to an empire that became more and more patently absurd as its days drew to an end. We see its local representative, the plumed district commissioner, reading His Majesty's inane speech on Empire Day— a man who had gone native at least as far as his women went, pursuing them in his numerous treks into the bush and leaving his sex-starved wife to carry the white man's burden in the starchy sterility of their district headquarters. We see the African spokesman replying to the royal address with a short bizarre speech ending suitably with an appeal for that symbol of hygienic progress, the pit latrine:

> Our people go to latrine in the bush. This is not good. We are happy to serve our noble and gracious King. God save the King.

Then we see poor Abotsi, minion of Empire, who has fought for King and imperial honour but goes mad on his return home because, presumably, he had neglected to perform a ritual of purification for all the Japs, enemies of Empire, he killed in Burma. When he is sick unto death the colonial hospital will not admit him, the spruce nurse complaining about people who smell like he-goats. The church —handmaiden of Empire—will not bury him either.

Another ex-serviceman, Sule, has also gone mad but is still in top physical form, marching every market day to his theme song of Burmese Days, drilling his five-year-old son in the merciless noonday heat.

So the death of Empire was not to be seriously lamented. Senile and absurd, it no longer had the will to stand by and protect its very own. But at least it had its heyday, its years of honour. Its successor, Independence, did not even wait to grow old before turning betrayer. That fine magical moonshaft whose image occurs again and again in the book, like some Freudian dream, the moonshaft which cleft the ocean (as Jehovah once parted the Red Sea so that His people might reach their land of freedom), soon degenerates into the obscene picture of a moon in a pee posture pissing into the sea. The cool milk bush (another recurrent image) around which the hero Amamu often walks to calm his exploding brain loses its coolness and catches fire:

> Stones, oil lamps, rings, landscape flashes, my milk bush is on fire, my people, it is on fire. The yellow lights of streets paved with human excrement from flying trucks pronounce and witness it.

Thus the disappearance of a beautiful and healing dream is witnessed by a sordid reality that abides.

In one way the whole allegory is a tortured return journey in search of a lost beginning:

> . . . let us return to the magic hour of our birth for which we mourn.
>
> Crowds came from every corner of the earth. The feast of oneness is here. They raised a shout to the sky, to the heavens, like the Israelites of old they have arrived on the shores of a promised land, like the Anlo sojourners they have come to a place of sunshine, of water, of fish and of good things of earth abundantly given, they must roll their mats and go no more. They have come home. Home is desolation, home is my anguish, home is my drink of hyssop and tears. Where is home?

Betrayal is central to the argument: betrayal of trust, of responsibility. It fouls all levels of a society that should have been dedicated to the restoration of its integrity. We see betrayal at the very top, by the very man who came to save; in the middle ranges by all those ridiculous professionals wasting their substance in drink and womanizing. At the lower reaches we see characters like Mr. Attipoe, the fat drunken road-overseer who orders the gates of Deme shut at the slightest hint of rain so that beleaguered lorry drivers would seek him out with bribes of his favourite illicit gin. Or Kodzo, the town crier, who drinks through seven wakes in two nights and forgets what message he should announce, although he has already taken his fee, his drink money of one shilling. He finally does remember after much effort of will; it is to tell Deme that the drunken overseer's sister has given birth to a child—a triviality that shows how traditional institutions and usages have been debased and travestied. But how could it be otherwise when traditional elders themselves, who should guard the customs, are in the front line of desecrators? Kodzo remembers them as

> . . . those stupid-looking old men, intensely looking at him, their gullets racing up and down in anticipation of the drink they would get from him. Especially Topa, his head like a Kuli water pot and eyes flaming like a parrot's tail feather. Never did an honest day's work. All he knew was to sit in judgment on others and get a drink out of them.

Through this teeming allegory we catch glimpses of the hero Amamu at significant moments in his life. The phrase "catch glimpses" is in fact misleading, since we know that even in those sequences that are most remote from him personally—for example, in the invocation of the poet killed in battle, Okigbo, or the assassinated freedom fighter, Eduardo Mondlane—it is Amamu who is stretched on the rack and also Africa whose story his life parallels in its purposelessness and self-destructiveness.

The question that one must ask at the end of Awoonor's book is: What then? He hasn't given any answer, and doesn't have to. But of late, many writers have been asking such questions: What then? What does Africa do? A return journey womb-wards to a rendezvous with golden-age innocence is clearly inadequate. Amamu's father may have acted insensitively, but on balance he was right to show impatience at all the lachrymose farewells before the boy's first departure from his mother's hut to the greater world beyond. Shoving aside the wailing women, he had brusquely and with a curse hoisted the boy into the lorry waiting to take him on a dusty journey to the coast and the future. The future is unavoidable. It has to be met. What is not inevitable is malingering purposelessness. Of that, even Ghanaians must now be prepared to acquit Nkrumah.

12

 Language
and the Destiny
 of Man

I N HIS LONG evolutionary history, man has scored few
greater successes than his creation of human society. For it is
on that primeval achievement that he has built those special
qualities of mind and of behaviour which, in his own view at
least, separate him from lower forms of life. If we sometimes
tend to overlook this fact it is only because we have lived so
long under the protective ambience of society that we have
come to take its benefits for granted. Which, in a way, might
be called the ultimate tribute; rather like the unspoken worship and thanksgiving which a man renders with every

Address first delivered at Dartmouth College, New Hampshire, in June 1972;
subsequently published in *Morning Yet on Creation Day*, Doubleday Anchor
Books, 1975.

breath he draws. If it were different we would not be men
but angels, incapable of boredom.

Unquestionably, language was crucial to the creation of
society. There is no way in which human society could exist
without speech. By society we do not, of course, mean the
mechanical and mindless association of the beehive or the
anthill which employs certain rudimentary forms of commu-
nication to achieve an unvarying, instinctual purpose, but a
community where man "doomed to be free"—to use Joyce
Cary's remarkable phrase—is yet able to challenge that peculiar and perilous destiny with an even chance of wresting
from it a purposeful, creative existence.

Speech too, like society itself, seems so natural that we
rarely give much thought to it or contemplate man's circumstance before its invention. But we know that language is not
inherent in man—the capacity for language, yes; but not
language. Therefore, there must have been a time in the very
distant past when our ancestors did not have it. Let us imagine a very simple incident in those days. A man strays into a
rock shelter without knowing that another is there finishing
a meal in the dark interior. The first hint our newcomer gets
of this fact is a loose rock hurled at his head. In a different
kind of situation which we shall call (with all kinds of guilty
reservations) *human,* that confrontation might have been resolved less destructively by the simple question: What do you
want? or even an angry: Get out of here!

Nobody is, of course, going to be so naïve as to claim for
language the power to dispose of all, or even most, violence.
After all, man is not less violent than other animals but more
—apparently the only animal which consistently visits violence on its own kind. Yet in spite of this (or perhaps because

of it) one does have a feeling that without language we should have long been extinct.

Many people following the fascinating progress of Dr. L. S. B. Leakey's famous excavations in the Olduvai Gorge in Eastern Africa in the 1950s were shocked by his claim that the so-called "pre-Zinjanthropus" child, the discovery of whose remains stirred many hearts and was one of the highlights of modern palaeontology, was probably murdered aged about twelve. Another excavator, Professor Raymond Dart, working further south, has collected much similar evidence of homicide in the caves of Transvaal.[1] But we should not have been surprised or shocked unless we had overlooked the psychological probability of the murder outside the Garden of Eden.

Let us take a second and quite different kind of example. Let us imagine an infant crying. Its mother assumes that it is hungry and offers it food; but it refuses to eat and goes on crying. Is it wet? Does it have pain? If so, where? Has an ant crawled into its dress and bitten it? Does it want to sleep? etc., etc. Thus the mother, especially if she lacks experience (as more and more mothers tend to do), will grope from one impulse to another, from one possibility to its opposite, until she stumbles on the right one. Meanwhile the child suffers distress and she mental anguish. In other words, because of a child's inadequate vocabulary even its simplest needs cannot be quickly known and satisfied. From which rather silly example we can see, I hope, the value of language in facilitating the affairs and transactions of society by enabling its members to pass on their message quickly and exactly.

In small closely-knit societies such as we often call primitive the importance of language is seen in pristine clarity. For instance, in the creation myth of the Hebrews, God made the

world by word of mouth; and in the Christian myth as recorded in St. John's Gospel the Word became God Himself.

African societies in the past held similar notions about
language and the potency of words. Writing about Igbo society in Nigeria, Igwe and Green had this to say:

> a speaker who could use language effectively and had a good com-
> mand of idioms and proverbs was respected by his fellows and was
> often a leader in the community.[2]

From another part of Africa a Kenyan, Mugo Gatheru, in
his autobiographical book gives even stronger testimony from
his people: "among the Kikuyu those who speak well have
always been honoured, and the very word chief means good
talker."[3]

There is a remarkable creation myth among the
Wapangwa people of Tanzania which begins thus:

> The sky was large, white, and very clear. It was empty; there were no
> stars and no moon; only a tree stood in the air and there was wind.
> This tree fed on the atmosphere and ants lived on it. Wind, tree, ants,
> and atmosphere were controlled by the power of the Word, but the
> Word was not something that could be seen. It was a force that en-
> abled one thing to create another.[4]

But although contemporary societies in Africa and elsewhere have moved away from beliefs and attitudes which
had invested language with such ritual qualities, we can still
find remains of the old dignity in certain places and circumstances. In his famous autobiography, Camara Laye records
the survival of such an attitude in the Guinea of his boyhood,
the strong impression that the traditional village could make
on the visitor from the town:

In everything, I noticed a kind of dignity which was often lacking in town life . . . And if their minds seemed to work slower in the country, that was because they always spoke only after due reflection, and because speech itself was a most serious matter.[5]

And finally, from a totally different environment, these lines of a traditional Eskimo poem, "Magic Words," from Jerome Rothenberg's excellent anthology, *Shaking the Pumpkin:*

> That was the time when words were like magic
> The human mind had mysterious powers.
> A word spoken by chance
> might have strange consequences.
> It would suddenly come alive
> and what people wanted to happen could happen—
> all you had to do was say it.[6]

In small and self-sufficient societies, such as gave birth to these myths, the integrity of language is safeguarded by the fact that what goes on in the community can easily be ascertained, understood and evaluated by all. The line between truth and falsehood thus tends to be sharp, and when a man addresses his fellows they know already what kind of person he is, whether (as Igbo people would put it) he is one with whose words something can be done; or else one who, if he tells you to stand, you know you must immediately flee!

But as society becomes larger and more complex we find that we can no longer be in command of all the facts but are obliged to take a good deal of what we hear on trust. We delegate to others the power to take certain decisions on our behalf, and they may not always be people we know or can vouch for. I shall return shortly to a consideration of this phenomenon. But first I shall consider a different, though

related, problem—the pressure to which language is sub-
jected by the mere fact that it can never change fast enough
to deal with every new factor in the environment, to describe
every new perception, every new detail in the ever-increasing
complexity of the life of the community, to say nothing of
the private perceptions and idiosyncrasies of particular speak-
ers. T. S. Eliot comes readily to mind with those memorable
lines from the *Four Quartets* in which he suggests to us the
constant struggle, frustration and anguish which this situation imposes on a poet:

> Trying to learn to use words, and every attempt
> Is a wholly new start, and a different kind of failure . . .[7]

Of course one might wonder whether this problem was a
real one for ordinary people like ourselves or a peculiar species of self-flagellation by a high-strung devotee seeking
through torment to become worthy of his deity. For when
Eliot goes on to celebrate the "sentence that is right" his
words do assume accents of holy intoxication:

> The common word exact without vulgarity,
> The formal word precise but not pedantic,
> The complete consort dancing together . . .[8]

This curious mix of high purpose and carnival jollity may
leave us a little puzzled, but there is no doubt whatever about
Eliot's concern and solicitude for the integrity of words. And
let us not imagine, even the most prosaic among us, that this
concern and the stringent practice Eliot advocates are appropriate only to poets. For we all stand to lose when language is
debased, just as every one of us is affected when the nation's
currency is devalued; not just the Secretary to the Treasury or
controllers of our banks.

Talking about Secretaries of the Treasury and devaluation, there was an amusing quotation by Professor Douglas Bush in an essay entitled "Polluting our Language" in the Spring 1972 issue of *The American Scholar*. The Secretary of the Treasury, John Connally, had said: "In the early sixties we were strong, we were virulent." Clearly, that was only a slip, albeit of a kind that might interest Freudians. But it might not be entirely unfair to see a tendency to devaluation inherent in certain occupations!

We must now turn from considering the necessary struggle with language arising, as it were, from its very nature and the nature of the society it serves to the more ominous threat to its integrity brought about neither by its innate inadequacy nor yet by the incompetence and carelessness of its ordinary users, but rather engineered deliberately by those who will manipulate words for their own ends.

It has long been known that language, like any other human invention, can be abused, can be turned from its original purpose into something useless or even deadly. George Orwell, who was very much concerned in his writings with this modern menace, reminds us that language can be used not only for expressing thought but for concealing thought or even preventing thought.[9] I guess we are all too familiar with this—from the mild assault of the sales pitch which exhorts you: "Be progressive! Use ABC toothpaste!" or invites you to a "saving spree" in a department store; through the mystifications of learned people jealously guarding the precincts of their secret societies with such shibboleths as: "Bilateral mastectomy was performed" instead of "Both breasts were removed";[10] to the politician who employs government prose to keep you in the dark about affairs on which your life or the lives of your children may depend or the official statistician who assures you that crime rates "are increasing at a decreasing rate of increase." I shall not waste your time about this well-known fact of modern life. But let me round off this aspect of the matter by quoting a little of the comment made by W. H. Auden in an interview published by the *New York Times* (19 October 1971):

> As a poet—not as a citizen—there is only one political duty, and that is to defend one's language from corruption. And that is particularly serious now. It's being so quickly corrupted. When it is corrupted people lose faith in what they hear, and this leads to violence.

And leads also full circle to the caveman situation with which we began. And the heart of my purpose is to suggest that our remote ancestors who made and preserved language for us, who, you might say, crossed the first threshold from bestiality to humanness, left us also adequate warning, wrapped in symbols, against its misuse.

Every people has a body of myths or sacred tales received from its antiquity. They are supernatural stories which man created to explain the problems and mysteries of life and death—his attempt to make sense of the bewildering complexity of existence. There is a proud, nomadic people, the Fulani, who inhabit the northern savannahs of Western Africa from Cameroon and Nigeria westwards to Mali and Senegal. They are very much attached to their cattle, whose milk is their staff of life. Here is a Fulani myth of creation from Mali:

> At the beginning there was a huge drop of milk.
> Then Doondari came and he created the stone.
> Then the stone created iron;
> And iron created fire;

And fire created water;
And water created air.

Then Doondari descended the second time.
And he took the five elements
And he shaped them into man.
But man was proud.
Then Doondari created blindness and blindness defeated man.
But when blindness became too proud,
Doondari created sleep, and sleep defeated blindness;
But when sleep became too proud,
Doondari created worry, and worry defeated sleep;
But when worry became too proud,
Doondari created death, and death defeated worry.

But when death became too proud,
Doondari descended for the third time,
And he came as Gueno, the eternal one
And Gueno defeated death.[11]

You notice, don't you, how in the second section of that
poem, after the creation of man, we have that phrase "became too proud" coming back again and again like the re-
currence of a dominant beat in rhythmic music? Clearly the
makers of that myth intended us not to miss it. So it was at
the very heart of their purpose. *Man is destroyed by pride.* It
is said over and over again; it is shouted like a message across
vast distances until the man at the other end of the savannah
has definitely got it, despite the noise of rushing winds. Or if
you prefer a modern metaphor, it is like making a long-
distance call when the line is faulty or in bad weather. You
shout your message and repeat it again and again just to
make sure.

Claude Lévi-Strauss, the French structural anthropologist, has indeed sought to explain the repetitive factor in myth in this way, relating it to general information theory. Our forefathers and ancestors are seen in the role of *senders* of the message; and we, the novices of society, as *receivers*.[12] The ancestors are sending us signals from the long history and experience of bygone days about the meaning of life, the qualities we should cultivate and the values that are important. Because they are so far away and because we are surrounded by the tumult and distractions of daily life they have to shout and repeat themselves not only in phrase after phrase but also in myth after myth, varying the form slightly now and again until the central message goes home.

If this interpretation is right then the Fulani myth of creation not only delivers a particular message on the danger of pride but also exemplifies beautifully the general intention and purpose of myths.

Let us now look at another short myth from the Igbo people in Nigeria which bears more directly on the question of language:

> When death first entered the world, men sent a messenger to Chuku, asking him whether the dead could not be restored to life and sent back to their old homes. They chose the dog as their messenger.
>
> The dog, however, did not go straight to Chuku, and dallied on the way. The toad had overheard the message, and as he wished to punish mankind, he overtook the dog and reached Chuku first. He said he had been sent by men to say that after death they had no desire at all to return to the world. Chuku declared that he would respect their wishes, and when the dog arrived with the true message he refused to alter his decision.
>
> Thus although a human being may be born again, he cannot return with the same body and the same personality.[13]

It has been pointed out that there are more than seven hundred different versions of this myth all over Africa. Thus, the element of repetition which we have seen in the form of a phrase recurring in time within one myth takes on the formidable power of spatial dispersion across a continent. Clearly the ancestral senders regard this particular signal as of desperate importance, hence its ubiquity and the profuse variations on its theme. Sometimes the messenger is the dog; sometimes the chameleon or the lizard, or some other animal. In some versions the message is garbled through the incompetence of the messenger, or through his calculated malice against man. In others, man in his impatience sends a second messenger to God who in anger withdraws the gift of immortality. But whatever variations in the detail the dominant theme remains: Men send a messenger to their Creator with a plea for immortality and He is disposed to grant their request. But something goes wrong with the message at the last moment. And this bounty which mankind has all but held in its grasp, this monumental gift that would have made man more like the gods, is snatched from him forever. And he knows that there is a way to hell even from the gates of heaven!

This, to my mind, is the great myth about language and the destiny of man. Its lesson should be clear to all. It is as though the ancestors who made language and knew from what bestiality its use rescued them are saying to us: Beware of interfering with its purpose! For when language is seriously interfered with, when it is disjoined from truth, be it from mere incompetence or worse, from malice, horrors can descend again on mankind.

13

 The Truth
of Fiction

P ICASSO once pronounced that all art was false. Since
the West gave him credit for something like 90 percent of its
twentieth-century artistic achievement, Picasso no doubt felt
free to say whatever he liked on the matter! Even so, I believe
he was merely drawing attention in the exaggerated manner
of seers and prophets to the important but simple fact that art
cannot be a carbon copy of life; and thus, in that specific
sense, cannot be "true." And if not true, it must therefore be
false!

But if art may dispense with the constraining exactitude of
literal truth, it does acquire in return incalculable powers of
persuasion in the imagination. Which was why a single can-

Convocation Lecture, University of Ife, 1978.

vas, *Guernica,* by Picasso himself could so frighten the state machinery of Spanish fascism. For how could a mere painting on canvas exercise such awe unless in some way it accorded with, or had a disquieting relationship to, recognizable reality? Unless, in other words, it spoke a kind of truth?

In his "Memorial Verses," Matthew Arnold put these words into the mouth of the poet and philosopher Goethe:

> The end is everywhere
> Art still has truth, take refuge there.[1]

Placed in that grand, apocalyptic setting, art and whatever truth is claimed for it are bound to become unduly remote.

Actually, art is man's constant effort to create for himself a different order of reality from that which is given to him; an aspiration to provide himself with a second handle on existence *through his imagination.* For practical considerations, I shall limit myself to just one of the forms he has fashioned out of his experience with language—the art of fiction.

In his brilliant essay *The Sense of an Ending,* Frank Kermode defines fiction simply as "something we know does not exist but which helps us to make sense of, and move in, the world."[2] Defining it in this practical way does prepare us not for one but for many varieties of fiction. Kermode himself draws attention to some of them, for example the mathematical fiction of "infinity plus one" which does not exist and yet facilitates the solution of certain problems in pure mathematics; or the legal fiction in certain legal systems which holds that when a man and his wife die at the same time the law, in pursuit of equity, will pretend that the woman dies before her husband, so that excessive hardship may not be brought upon their estate.

In other words, we invent different fictions to help us out

of particular problems we encounter in living. But of course these problems are not always as specific and clear-cut, or indeed as consciously perceived, as the lawyer's or the mathematician's formulations. When two very young children say to each other, "Let us pretend . . ." and begin to act such roles as father and mother they are obviously creating a fiction for a less definite, more spontaneous and, I dare say, more profound purpose.

What is the nature of this purpose? I don't think anyone can say for certain. All that we do know is that judging from the evidence of man's fiction-making in all places and at all times he must surely have an inescapable need for that activity. No one has yet come upon the slightest evidence that any human group now or in the past managed to dispense with the need to make fictions.

Given the great gulf between being and knowing, between his essence and existence, man has no choice really but to make and believe in some fiction or other. Perhaps the ultimate judgement on a man is not whether he acquiesces to a fiction but rather what *kind* of fiction will persuade him into that acquiescence, that willing suspension of disbelief which Coleridge spoke about or that "experimental submission," to quote I. A. Richards.

However, we must not overlook the carefulness displayed by both Coleridge and Richards in their choice of words; and for a very good reason. Coleridge's disbelief is only *suspended,* not abolished, and will presumably return at the appropriate moment; and Richards's submission is experimental, not definitive or permanent.

It is important to stress this point because man makes not only fictions to which he gives guarded or temporary acquiescence like the pretending games of healthy children; he has the capacity also to create fictions that demand and indeed impose upon him absolute and unconditional obedience. I will shortly return to this, but first of all let me extend what I have said about man's desire for fictions to include the question of his capacity. Man's desire for fictions goes with his ability for making them, just as his need for language is inseparable from his capacity for speech. If man only had the need to speak but lacked his peculiar speech organs, he could not have invented language. For all we know, other animals in the jungle might be in just as much need to talk to one another as man ever was and might have become just as eloquent had they been endowed with the elaborate apparatus for giving expression to that need. And certainly no one would suggest that the mute is silent because he has no need to speak or nothing to say. If we apply the same reasoning to man's propensity for fictions we can see that his need to create them would not adequately explain their existence; there must also be an effective apparatus.

This equipment, I suggest, is man's imagination. For just as man is a tool-making animal and has recreated his natural world with his tools, so is he a fiction-making animal and refashions his imaginative landscape with his fictions.

All attempts to define man neatly must fail because of his complexity. Man is a rational animal; man is a political animal; man is a tool-making animal, man is etc., etc. If you ask me I will add that man is a questioning animal, a highly curious animal. Given his mental and imaginative capacities this curiosity is only to be expected. Man finds himself caught, as it were, in a tiny glow-worm of consciousness. Behind him is the impenetrable darkness of his origin, and before him is another deep obscurity into which he seems headed. What is shrouded by those darknesses? What is the meaning of this tiny, intervening spot of light which is his earthly existence? In the face of these mysteries man's capacities are at once immense and severely circumscribed. His knowledge though impressive and expanding will never in all likelihood match what he needs to know. Not even the accumulated knowledge and wisdom of all his species will suffice. The ultimate questions will in all probability remain.

In the 1950s a Nigerian microbiologist, Dr. Sanya Onabamiro, published a book which he entitled, with great perspicacity, *Why Our Children Die,* echoing what must have been one of the most poignant and heartrending questions asked by our ancestors down the millennia. Why do our children die? Being a modern scientist Dr. Onabamiro gave appropriate twentieth-century answers: disease, undernourishment and ignorance. Every reasonable person will accept that this "scientific" answer is more satisfactory than answers we might be given from other quarters. For example, a witch doctor might tell us that our children die because they are bewitched; because someone else in the family has offended a god or, in some other secret way, erred. Some years ago I watched the pitiful spectacle of an emaciated little child brought out and sat on a mat in the midst of the desperate *habitués* of a prayer-house while the prophetess with maniacal authority pronounced it possessed by the devil and ordered its parents to fast for seven days.

The point of these examples is to suggest two things: first, the richness, the sheer prodigality, of man's inventiveness in creating aetiological fictions; second, that not all his fictions are equally useful or desirable.

But first of all I must explain my temerity in thus appearing to lump together under the general rubric of fictions the cool, methodical and altogether marvellous procedures of modern medicine with the erratic "visions" of a religious psychopath. In all truth, the two ought never to be mentioned in the same breath. And yet they share, however remotely it may seem, the same need of man to explain and alleviate his intolerable condition. And they both make use of theories of disease—the germ theory, on the one hand, and the theory of diabolical possession, on the other. And theories are no more than fictions which help us to make sense of experience and which are subject to disconfirmation when their explanations are no longer adequate. There is no doubt, for instance, that scientists in the twenty-first and later centuries will look at some of the most cherished scientific notions of our day with the same amused indulgence that we show towards the fumblings of past generations.

And yet we can say, indeed we must say, that the insights given by Dr. Onabamiro into the problem of high infant mortality, however incomplete future generations may find them, are infinitely more helpful to us than the diagnosis of a half-mad religious fanatic. In conclusion, there are fictions that help and fictions that hinder. For simplicity, let us call them beneficent and malignant fictions.

What is it then about fictions—good or bad—that makes them so appealing? Why does man have to take leave of reality in order to ease his passage through the real world? What lies behind this apparent paradox? Why is the imagination so powerful that it lures us so constantly away from the animal existence that our physical senses will impose on us?

Let me frame these questions somewhat differently so that we may not fly off at a tangent and get lost altogether in the heady clouds of abstraction.

Why does Amos Tutuola's *The Palm-Wine Drinkard* offer us a better, stronger and more memorable insight into the problem of excess than all the sermons and editorials we have heard and read, or will hear and read, on the same subject?

The reason is that while editorials and other preachments may tell us all about excess, Tutuola performs the miracle of transforming us into active participants in a powerful drama of the imagination in which excess in all its guises takes on flesh and blood. Afterwards we can no longer act as hearers only of the word; we are initiates; we have made our visit; we have encountered ourselves in the Drinkard in much the same way as the Drinkard has encountered himself in the course of a corrective quest—albeit unknowingly—in that preposterous clump of unpleasantness that is his own son, the half-bodied baby. The encounter like much else in the novel is made unforgettable for us because of Tutuola's inventiveness not only in revealing the variety of human faces that excess may wear, but also in his deft exploration of the moral and philosophical consequences of breaching, through greed, the law of reciprocity which informs like a gravitational force the seemingly aberratic motions of his bizarre, fictive universe.

This self-encounter which I consider the major source of the potency and success of beneficent fictions may be defined also as imaginative identification. Things are then not merely happening *before* us; they are happening, by the power and force of imaginative identification, *to* us. We not only see; we *suffer* alongside the hero and are branded with the same mark of "punishment and poverty," to use Tutuola's familiar phrase.

Thus, without having to undergo personally the ordeals which the Drinkard has to suffer in atonement for his idleness and lack of self-control we become, through an act of our imagination, beneficiaries of his regenerative adventure.

That we are able to do this is one of the greatest boons to our reflective humanity—the capacity to experience *directly* the highway on which we are embarked and also, *vicariously,* "the road not taken," as Robert Frost might say.

Given our questioning nature the end of which is discovery, and given our existential limitations especially the vastness of our ignorance, one can begin to appreciate the immeasurable blessing that our imagination could confer on us. It is a truism and a cliché that experience is the best teacher; it is even arguable whether we can truly *know* anything which we have not personally experienced. But our imagination can narrow the existential gap by giving us in a wide range of human situations the closest approximation to experience that we are ever likely to get, and sometimes the safest too, as anyone who has travelled on Nigerian roads can tell you! For it is hardly desirable to be run over by a car in order to *know* that automobiles are dangerous. We can learn from that battered corpse by the roadside; not simply by observing it but by creating the chastening fiction *that we are it,* that the corpse of another man is *not,* as an Igbo proverb would have it, a log of wood, but ourselves. (Except that on further reflection that proverb is not in fact the outrageous thing I have just said. Another man's corpse *seems to us* like a log of wood, is what it says—a rather different matter and a very sad reflection on our impaired imagination, on our malfunctioning powers of identification with the plight of our fellows.)

Life is short and art is long, said the ancients. We can mitigate the brevity of the one with the longevity of the other. This is why human societies have always attempted to sustain their cultural values by carefully preserved oral or written literatures which provide for them and their posterity a short cut now and again to the benefits of actual experience. What about history, you might ask, does it not vouchsafe the same enlightenment? The lessons of history are important, of course. But think how many aeons of history will be needed to distil the wisdom of Shakespeare's *King Lear.* And in any case, what great solace can many of us recent colonials derive from an effective history which is so nasty, British and short?

For a society to function smoothly and effectively its members must share certain basic tenets of belief and norms of behaviour. There must be a reasonable degree of consensus on what is meant by virtue and vice; there must be some agreement on the attributes of a hero, on what constitutes the heroic act. Different societies will not hold identical ideas on these questions in every part of the world or at every time in history. And yet, in spite of local and historical variations, we do not know of any society which has survived and flourished on totally arbitrary notions of good and evil, or of the heroic and the cowardly. Our very humanity seems to be committed to a distinction between these pairs however fuzzy the line may sometimes appear. But a society, like an individual, can sicken or become unhinged mentally, as in the phenomenon of mass hysteria which is well known. There are, of course, quieter and less dramatic symptoms of social pathology. Vulgar ostentation, callousness, disorderliness, filth and shoddiness are clear signs of disease. What is the cure? More exhortations? I think not.

The great virtue of literary fiction is that it is able by engaging our imagination to lead us "to discovery and recognition by an unexpected and instructive route,"[3] in the words of Kermode. It helps us locate again the line between the heroic and the cowardly when it seems most shadowy and elusive, and it does this by forcing us to encounter the heroic and the cowardly in our own pysche.

How often do we hear people say, "Oh I don't have the time to read novels," implying that fiction is frivolous? They would generally add—lest you consider them illiterate—that they read histories or biographies, which they presume to be more appropriate to serious-minded adults. Such people are to be pitied; they are like a six-cylinder car which says: Oh, I can manage all right on three sparking-plugs, thank you very much. Well, it can manage somehow but it will sound like an asthmatic motorcycle!

The life of the imagination is a vital element of our total nature. If we starve it or pollute it the quality of our life is depressed or soiled.

We must not, however, celebrate the beauties of imagination and the beneficent fictions that are spun in its golden looms without mentioning the terrible danger to which it can be exposed.

Belief in superior and inferior races; belief that some people who live across our frontiers or speak a different language from ourselves are the cause of all the trouble in the world, or that our own particular group or class or caste has a right to certain things which are denied to others; the belief that men are superior to women, and so on—all are fictions generated by the imagination. What then makes them different from the beneficent fiction for which I am making rather large claims? One might reply: By their fruits, ye shall know them. Logically that may be a good answer, but strategically it is inadequate. For it might imply that Hitler should first commit genocide before we can conclude that racism is a horrendous evil, or that South Africa should go up in flames to confirm it. So we must find a criterion with an alarm system that screams red whenever we begin to spin virulent fictions.

Such an early-warning system is ready to hand and really quite simple. You remember the example of the children at play, how they preface their little drama by saying, "Let us pretend." What distinguishes beneficent fiction from such malignant cousins as racism is that the first never forgets that it is fiction and the other never knows that it is. Literary fiction does not ask us to believe, for instance, that the Palm-Wine Drinkard actually drank one hundred and fifty kegs of palm wine every morning and seventy-five kegs in the evening, that he underwent the adventure so vividly described in the novel or indeed that he even existed. And yet reading the novel explains so much to us and affects radically the way we perceive the world thereafter.

Malignant fictions like racial superiority, on the other hand, never say, "Let us pretend." They assert their fictions as a proven fact and a way of life. Holders of such fictions are really like lunatics, for while a sane person might act a play now and again, a madman lives it permanently. Some people would describe malignant fictions as myths, but I find no justification for soiling the reputation of myths in that way. I would prefer to call malignant fictions by their proper name, which is superstitions. But whatever we call them, it is essential to draw a clear distinction between beneficent fiction and any arbitrary nonsense emanating from a sick imagination. Watching a magician and marvelling at his sleight of hand and management of optical tricks is something quite different from seeing him and *believing* that his powers derive from midnight visits to cemeteries or from reading the Sixth and Seventh Books of Moses. Beneficent fiction operates within the bounds of imagination; superstition breaks the bounds and ravages the real world.

We are totally wrong when we imagine that self-centredness is smart. It is actually very stupid, an indication that we lack enough imagination to recreate in ourselves the thoughts that must go on in the minds of others, especially those we dispossess. A person who is insensitive to the suffering of his fellows is that way because he lacks the imaginative power to get under the skin of another human being and see the world through eyes other than his own. History and fiction are replete with instances of correlation between indifference and lack of imagination. Think of the aristocratic lady who was driving home to her estate one winter evening and saw through the shutterless windows of a wretched hut a boy shivering in rags.

Moved to pity, she said to her coachman, "Remark that hut, for as soon as I get home I must send warm things to that poor boy."

When she got home and sat in front of a huge, crackling fire her coachman came to her and said, "Madam, about the poor boy . . ."

"Oh, but it's nice and warm again," she replied.

Think of the Queen of France before the French Revolution who was told that the people had no bread to eat and she said, "Well, let them eat cake." It is generally thought that she was a heartless monster. More likely she was only a pathetic, stupid woman who genuinely believed that if people were out of bread they should be able to manage with cake until they could stock up again.

Privilege, you see, is one of the great adversaries of the imagination; it spreads a thick layer of adipose tissue over our sensitivity.

We see the same deadening of consciousness all around us today at all levels—personal, communal, national and international. Not so long ago I saw a startling sight right under a multi-million-*naira* flyover in Lagos. A beggar was crouching in the middle of the road scooping something into a bowl while furious cars dodged him on all sides. As we got close I realized that the brownish-white stuff he was collecting was not pure sand but a mixture of sand and salt. A salt bag must have fallen out of a van and broken there and he had come on the scene rather late. The friend driving me said, "This is one Nigerian whom the oil boom missed." I could not get over the gigantic, almost crude, irony of that scene: the multi-million-dollar modern bridge overhead, a beggar defying instant death to scoop sand into a bowl for his soup. I recalled a poem I had just received for the *Okike* magazine, "The Romance of Beggars":

> We want risk capital
> Not beggars
> Social overhead capital
> Not a begging bowl
> Don't rattle it
> Don't rattle your begging bowl in
> this economy.

Later, in another sequence of the same poem, a hot-blooded beggar, living as many do in Lagos, prehistorically in concrete caves below modern bridges, gives out this invitation:

> Come here into the hollow of my conscience
> I will show you a thing or two
> I will show you the heat of my love.
> You know what?

> I can give you babies too
> Real leaders of tomorrow
> Right here under the bridge
> I can give you real leaders of thought.

I don't think that elegant Miss Nigeria will have the imagination or conscience to explore the possibilities of that encounter. She will dodge the rude beggar and speed away in her expensive car to a sterile assignation with her bloated Mr. Overhead Capital.

No, indifference to suffering is not clever at all. The late Hannah Arendt showed real perceptiveness when she called her study of the psychology of totalitarianism *The Banality of Evil.*

Imaginative identification is the opposite of indifference; it is human connectedness at its most intimate. It is one step better than the golden rule: Do unto others . . . Our sense of that link is the great social cement that really holds, and it will manifest itself in fellow-feeling, justice and fair play. My theory of the uses of fiction is that beneficent fiction calls into full life our total range of imaginative faculties and gives us a heightened sense of our personal, social and human reality. One thing that worries one above all else in the frenetic materialism that pervades our contemporary life is that as a species we may be losing the Open Sesame to the *mundo* of fiction—that ability to say "Let us pretend" like grace before our act; and to say "Our revels now are ended" like a benediction when we have finished—and *yet* to draw from this insubstantial pageant essential insights and wisdoms for making our way in the real world. The supple articulation of our imagination seems, alas, to be hardening rapidly into the sclerotic rigidity of literal-mindedness and material concerns.

An English friend, a marvellous raconteur at dinner, had just told a group of us of an anxious flight he and his wife recently made from the Far East when it occurred to his wife to ask him, by the way, if he had taken out flight insurance on that trip. "Oh yes," he replied blithely, "if the plane had crashed we would have been the richest couple in the cemetery." A few days later I repeated the joke to a doctor friend, who retorted promptly and unsmilingly that the money would have been paid to their next of kin. I thought: Oh my God, what a fate to befall the descendants of those incomparable fabulists who made our great oral traditions!

And I began to think of that other and far more serious experience which I had. I wrote a social satire called *A Man of the People,* which was published in January 1966, as fate would have it, two days after Nigeria's first military coup. Because the novel ends also with a military coup a certain degree of surprise and conjecture and, I might add, admiration was inevitable among my readers. What was not inevitable, however, was the theory which grew apparently during the civil war in certain quarters that because I wrote the novel I must have been one of the planners of the military coup. Long after the civil war I was questioned rather closely on this matter after I had given a lecture in one of our universities. Rather annoyed, I asked my questioner if he had read the book and he said vaguely yes. Did he remember, I asked him then, that before the coup in my story there was first a blatant rigging of an election, civil commotion in the land, murder and arson, which happened to be paralleled also by similar events in Nigeria before the January coup. Was he suggesting that I too planned those upheavals in Ibadan and elsewhere? Did he remember that my story specifically mentions a counter-coup, a prophecy which, alas, was also fulfilled in Nigeria in July 1966. Was he suggesting that I sat in on the planning of that as well? In general, did he think that a group of dissident army officers planning to overthrow their government would invite a novelist to sit in on their plot, go back to their barracks and wait for two years while the novelist wrote up the book, had it edited and produced by his publishers, and only then spring into action and effect their coup to coincide with the book's publication? Such a theory might have been excusable in 1966 for the armed soldiers who had gone in search of me first to my office and then, fortunately, to a house I had already vacated. How could they know that the offending book had taken two years to write and publish? But a university teacher in 1977!

This lengthy personal anecdote would not be necessary if it did not show more clearly than almost anything I have direct experience of how easy it is for us to short-circuit the power of our imagination by our own act of will. For when a desperate man wishes to believe something however bizarre or stupid, nobody can stop him. He will discover in his imagination a willing and enthusiastic accomplice. Together they will weave the necessary fiction which will then bind him securely to his cherished intention.

The fiction which imaginative literature offers us is not like that. It does not enslave; it liberates the mind of man. Its truth is not like the canons of an orthodoxy or the irrationality of prejudice and superstition. It begins as an adventure in self-discovery and ends in wisdom and humane conscience.

14

What Has Literature
Got to Do with It?

MAN is a goal-setting animal. Alone or in concert with his fellows he does frequently tend to select and tackle his problems in graded priorities. He identifies personal goals, family goals, community goals, national and international goals; and he focuses his attention on solving them. At the national level, for example, he has invented short-term annual budgets and long-term five- or ten-year development plans; and, for good measure, we do have in this country chiliastic expectations such as health for all in the magic year of 2000.

Setting goals is a matter of intelligence and judgement. Faced with a confusing welter of problems all clamouring for

Nigerian National Merit Award Lecture given at Sokoto on 23 August 1986.

solution at once, man's most rational strategy is to stay as cool as possible in the face of the confusion and attack the problems singly or in small manageable groups, one at a time. Of course the choice of what he must assault first or what he can reserve for last is of the utmost importance and can determine his success or failure.

The comprehensive goal of a developing nation like Nigeria is, of course, development, or its somewhat better variant, modernization. I don't see much room for argument about that. What can be, and is, vigorously debated is the quickest and safest route for the journey into modernization and what items should make up the traveller's rather limited baggage allowance.

But the problem with goals lies not only in the area of priorities and practicalities. There are appropriate and inappropriate goals, even wrong and unworthy goals. There are goals which place an intolerable strain on the pursuer. History tells us, for example, of leaders who in their obsessive pursuit of modernization placed on their people such pressures as they were unable to bear—Peter the Great of Russia, Muhammad Ali of Egypt and others. Out of contemporary China rumours have come that the national goal of the one-child family which was set to combat a disastrous population problem has come into conflict with the desire of ordinary rural parents for male children and has apparently led to the large-scale secret murder of female children. It is clear from these and similar examples that a nation might set itself a goal that puts its very soul at risk.

At the Tokyo Colloquium in October 1981, under the theme of Diversified Evolution of World Civilization, Professor Marion J. Levy of Princeton University, known for his study of the history of modernization in Japan and China, made the following remark about Japan:

> Well over half a century ago when everyone else was occupied with describing Japan in terms of the warrior and merchant classes Yanagida Kunio took the position that the real heart of Japan was in the customs of the Japanese farmer.[1]

If Kunio was right the point made by Professor Levy is very instructive. The mercantile and militaristic (but particularly the militaristic) goals of Japan in the first half of this century would then seem to have been at variance with the real heart of Japan—or perhaps one should say that the heart of Japan was not fully in them. This is of course an area of discourse where firm proof and certainty would be unattainable. But I think that Kunio's view does gain credence from the fact that Japan, whose celebrated militarism suffered one of the most horrendous defeats ever visited on an army in modern, or indeed any, times, was yet able to survive and muster the morale to become in twenty-odd years a miracle of technological and economic success, outstripping all comers. A very colourful metaphor comes readily to mind—snatching victory out of the jaws of defeat.

The history of Nigeria from, say, 1970 to 1983 can be characterized by contrast as a snatching of defeat from the jaws of victory, if one considers how nearly 100,000 million *naira* went through our hands like so much sand through the fingers of a child at play on the beach. How do we begin to explain that? Did we not have goals? Did we not have development plans? Did we not have experts to guide our steps on the slippery slopes of modernization?

But we did have all those things—annual budgets, development plans, the lot. We were not short on experts, either.

If we didn't have the particular kind we required, surely we had the money to hire him. What went wrong then? Our heart? Our mind? It seems our heart was not in it. Perhaps we suffered a failure of imagination. Perhaps psychologically we did not really wish to become a modern state; we saw the price of modernization and subconsciously decided we were not prepared to pay it.

Let us examine one or two of these suppositions, beginning with the question of the expert. No nation which contemplates modernization can neglect the role of the expert. He is needed; he must be paid for and he must be given adequate protection of tenure as well as respect so that others inferior to him may be motivated to strive and attain his expertise rather than hope through cheap politicking to manoeuvre themselves into his seat.

But having an expert among us does not absolve the rest of us from thinking. To begin with, the expert is generally an expert only in a narrow specialism. He can build a bridge for us perhaps, and tell us what weight of traffic it can support. But he can't stop us from hiring an attendant who will take a bribe and look the other way while the prescribed weight is exceeded. He can set up the finest machinery for us, but he can't create the technician who will stay at his post and watch the controls instead of going for a chat and some groundnuts under a mango tree outside.

So there is a limit to what an expert can do for us. In 1983, just before the overthrow of President Shagari's administration, I gave an interview for a television programme which subsequently caused some offence in certain quarters. One of the questions put to me was what did I think about the President's Green Revolution programme. And I said then, as I would say today, that it was a disaster which gave us plenty of food for thought and nothing at all in our stomach. Whereupon a certain fellow with a lot of grouse in him wrote in the papers that I should not have been asked to comment on agriculture because I was not an expert in that field. Well, we don't really need a Ph.D. in agriculture to tell us when our stomach is empty, do we? If we are in reasonable health we should all carry around with us reliable, inbuilt alarm systems popularly called hunger to apprise us of our condition!

I must say in this regard that the best experts do not themselves encourage us to have foolish and superstitious faith in their ability to solve our diverse development problems. In an essay published by the *American Economic Review* in 1984 Sir Arthur Lewis, one of the foremost development economists in the world and no stranger by any means to problems of African underdevelopment, did highlight in his inimitably elegant fashion the sheer plethora of prescriptions among development experts of differing persuasions:

> Every school has offered its own candidate for driver of the engine of growth. The physiocrats, agriculture; the Mercantilists, an export surplus; the classicists, the free market; the Marxists, capital; the neoclassicists, entrepreneurship; the Fabians, government; the Stalinists, industrialization; and the Chicago School, schooling.[2]

To sum up this marvellous passage I have composed a couplet which I beg pardon to inflict on you:

> There! we have it on the best authority
> Theorists of development cannot agree!

I will turn now to another world-famous economist, John Kenneth Galbraith, for a different kind of testimony. Interestingly, John Kenneth Galbraith is the current President of the American Academy of Arts and Letters. I must crave your indulgence to quote a fairly long extract from his address to the Academy in 1984 about the role of the arts in industry:

> Finally let no one minimize the service that the arts render to established industry. In the years since World War II . . . there has been no economic miracle quite like that of Italy. That lovely country has gone from one political disaster to another with one of the highest rates of economic growth of any of the industrial lands. The reason is not that the Italian government is notably precise in its administration, that Italian engineers and scientists are better than others, that Italian management is inspired or that Italian trade unions are more docile than the AFL-CIO. The Italian success derives from the Italian artistic tradition. Italian products over the widest range are superior not in durability, not in engineering excellence, not in lower cost. They are better in design. Italian design and the consequent industrial success are the result of centuries of recognition of—including *massive subsidy* to—the arts.

In concluding his address, Galbraith made the following affirmation:

> The arts are not the poor relation of the economic world. On the contrary they are at the very source of its vitality.[3]

Before I leave these foreign references I must return very briefly to that other miracle, Japan, to which I have already made reference. If "there has been no economic miracle quite like that of Italy," there has been none to match Japan's in dramatic suddenness and awesomeness of scale. It has been uniquely salutary also for thoroughly debunking all the bogus mystique summoned to explain Western industrialism— the Protestant ethic, the Graeco-Judaic tradition, etc. We, the latecomers (as Marion J. Levy calls us), have every reason to pay special attention to Japan's success story as we take our faltering steps to modernization.

In the 1981 Tokyo Colloquium which I spoke about earlier we were attempting, among other things, to define the cultural ingredient, or as one of the Japanese scholars put it the "software," of modernization. One of the observations that made a particularly strong impact on me in this connection was a little family anecdote by Professor Kinichiro Toba of Waseda University:

> My grandfather graduated from the University of Tokyo at the beginning of the 1880s. His notebooks were full of English. My father graduated from the same university in 1920 and half of his notes were filled with English. When I graduated a generation later my notes were all in Japanese. So . . . it took three generations for us to consume western civilization totally via the means of our own language.[4]

If Professor Toba's story is at all typical of the last 100 years of Japanese history (and we have no reason to believe otherwise), we can conclude that as Japan began the countdown to its spectacular technological lift-off it was also systematically recovering lost ground in its traditional mode of cultural expression. In one sense then it was travelling away from its old self towards a cosmopolitan, modern identity, while in another sense it was journeying back to regain a threatened past and selfhood. To comprehend the dimensions of this gigantic paradox and coax from it such unparalleled inventiveness requires not mere technical flair but the archaic energy, the perspective, the temperament of creation myths and symbolism.

It is in the very nature of creativity, in its prodigious complexity and richness, that it will accommodate paradoxes and ambiguities. But this, it seems, will always elude and pose a problem for the uncreative, *literal* mind (which I hasten to add is not the same as the *literary* mind, nor even the merely *literate* mind). The literal mind is the one-track mind, the simplistic mind, the mind that cannot comprehend that where one thing stands, another will stand beside it—the mind (finally and alas!) which appears to dominate our current thinking on Nigeria's need for technology.

The cry all around is for more science and less humanities (for in the narrow disposition of the literal mind more of one must mean less of the other). Our older universities have been pressured into a futile policy of attempting to allocate places on a 60:40 ratio in favour of science admissions. In addition, we have rushed to create universities of technology (and just as promptly proceeded to shut down half of them again) to demonstrate our priorities as well as confusions.

Nobody doubts that the modern developed world owes much of its success to scientific education and development. There is no doubt either that a nation can decide to emphasize science in its educational programme in order to achieve a specific national objective. When the Russians put the first man in orbit in 1961, John Kennedy responded by doubling United States space appropriations in 1962 and intensified a programme of space research which was to land Americans on the moon within the decade. But Kennedy did not ask the universities to starve out America's liberal arts education. As a matter of fact he had previously demonstrated sufficient awareness of the national need for the arts when at his inauguration he broke with tradition and gave pride of place to a reading by Robert Frost, the great New England poet.

Furthermore, it is important to realize that because a country like America with a well-developed and viable educational system may safely switch emphases around in its educational programme it does not therefore follow that Nigeria, whose incipient programme is already in a shambles, can do the same. What kind of science can a child learn in the absence, for example, of basic language competence and an attendant inability to handle concepts?

Have we reflected on the fact that in pre-independence Nigeria the only schools equipped adequately to teach science, namely the four or five government colleges, not only produced doctors and engineers like other schools but held an almost complete monopoly in producing novelists, poets and playwrights?

Surely if this fact proves anything it is that education is a complex creative process and the more rounded it is the more productive it will become.[5] It is not a machine into which you feed raw materials at one end and pick up packaged products at the other. It is, indeed, like creativity itself, "a many-splendoured thing."

The great nineteenth-century American poet Walt Whitman has left us a magnificent celebration of the many-sided nature of the creative spirit:

> Do I contradict myself?
> Very well then I contradict myself
> (I am large, I contain multitudes) . . .

The universal creative rondo revolves on people and stories. *People create stories create people;* or rather, *stories create people create stories.* Was it stories first and then people, or the other way round? Most creation myths would seem to suggest the antecedence of stories—a scenario in which the story was already unfolding in the cosmos before, and even as a result of which, man came into being. Take the remarkable Fulani creation story (see page 134):

In the beginning there was a huge drop of milk. Then the milk created stone; the stone created fire; the fire created water; the water created air.

Then Doondari came and took the five elements and moulded them into man. But man was proud. Then Doondari created blindness and blindness defeated man . . .

A fabulously rich story, it proceeds in stark successions of creation and defeat to man's death through hubris, and then to a final happy twist of redemption when death itself, having inherited man's arrogance, causes Doondari to descend a third time as Gueno the eternal one, to defeat death.

So important have such stories been to mankind that they are not restricted to accounts of initial creation but will be found following human societies as they recreate themselves through vicissitudes of their history, validating their social organizations, their political systems, their moral attitudes and religious beliefs, even their prejudices. Such stories serve the purpose of consolidating whatever gains a people or their leaders have made or imagine they have made in their existential journey through the world; but they also serve to sanction change when it can no longer be denied. At such critical moments new versions of old stories or entirely fresh ones tend to be brought into being to mediate the changes and sometimes to consecrate opportunistic defections into more honourable rites of passage.

One of the paradoxes of Igbo political systems is the absence of kings on the one hand, and on the other the presence in the language and folklore of a whole range of words for "king" and all the paraphernalia of royalty. In the Igbo town of Ogidi where I grew up I have found two explanatory myths offered for the absence of kings. One account has

it that once upon a time the title of king did exist in the
community but that it gradually fell out of use because of the
rigorous condition it placed on the aspirant, requiring him to
settle the debt owed by every man and every woman in the
kingdom.

The second account has it that there was indeed a king,
who held the people in such utter contempt that one day
when he had a ritual kola-nut to break for them he cracked it
between his teeth. So the people, who did not fancy eating
kola-nut coated with the king's saliva, dethroned him and
have remained republican ever since.

These are perhaps no more than fragmentary makeshift
accounts though not entirely lacking in allegorical interest.
There is, for instance, a certain philosophical appropriateness
to the point that a man who would be king over his fellows
should in return be prepared personally to guarantee their
solvency.

Be that as it may, those two interesting fragments of republican propaganda played their part in keeping kings'
noses out of the affairs of Ogidi for as long as memory could
go until the community, along with the rest of Nigeria, lost
political initiative to the British at the inception of colonial
rule. Thereafter a new dynasty of kings rose to power in
Ogidi with the connivance of the British administration, thus
rendering those mythical explanations of republicanism obso-
lete. Except perhaps that they may have left a salutary, mod-
erating residue in the psyche of the new rulers and those they
ruled.

I shall now, with your indulgence, present two brief para-
bles from pre-colonial Nigeria which are short enough for
the present purpose but also complex enough to warrant my
classifying them as literature. I chose these two particularly

because they stand at the opposite ends of the political spectrum.

> Once upon a time, all the animals were summoned to a meeting. As they converged on the public square early in the morning one of them, the fowl, was spotted by his neighbours going in the opposite direction. They said to him, "How is it that you are going away from the public square? Did you not hear the town crier's summons last night?"
>
> "I did hear it," said the fowl, "and I should certainly have gone to the meeting if a certain personal matter had not cropped up which I must attend to. I am truly sorry, but I hope you will make my sincere apologies to the meeting. Tell them that though absent in body I will be there with you in spirit in all your deliberations. Needless to say that whatever you decide will receive my whole-hearted support."
>
> The question before the assembled animals was what to do in the face of a new threat posed by man's frequent slaughtering of animals to placate his gods. After a stormy but surprisingly brief debate it was decided to present to man one of their number as his regular sacrificial animal if he would leave the rest in peace. And it was agreed without a division that the fowl should be offered to man to mediate between him and his gods. And it has been so ever since.

The second story goes like this:

> One day a snake was riding his horse coiled up, as was his fashion, in the saddle. As he came down the road he met the toad walking by the roadside.
>
> "Excuse me, sir," said the toad, "but that's not the way to ride a horse."
>
> "Really? Can you show me the right way, then?" asked the snake.
>
> "With pleasure, if you will be good enough to step down a moment."
>
> The snake slid down the side of his horse and the toad jumped with alacrity into the saddle, sat bolt upright and galloped most elegantly up

and down the road. "That's how to ride a horse," he said at the end of his excellent demonstration.

"Very good," said the snake, "very good indeed; you may now come down."

The toad jumped down and the snake slid up the side of his horse back into the saddle and coiled himself up as before. Then he said to the toad, "Knowing is good, but having is better. What good does fine horsemanship do to a fellow without a horse?" And then he rode away in his accustomed manner.[6]

On the face of it, those are just two charming animal stories to put a smile on the face or, if we are fortunate and have a generous audience, even a laugh in the throat. But beneath that admittedly important purpose of giving delight there lies a deep and very serious intent. Indeed, what we have before us are political and ideological statements of the utmost consequence revealing more about the societies that made and sustained them, and by which, in the reciprocal rondo of creativity, they were made and sustained, revealing far more than any number of political-science monographs could possibly ever tell us. We could literally spend hours analysing each story and discovering new significances all the time. Right now, however, we can take only a cursory look.

Consider the story of the delinquent fowl. Quite clearly it is a warning, a cautionary tale, about the danger to which citizens of small-scale democratic systems may be exposed when they neglect the cardinal duty of active participation in the political process. In such systems a man who neglects to lick his lips, as a certain proverb cautions us, will be asking the harmattan to lick them for him. It did for the fowl with a vengeance!

The second story is, if you will permit a rather predictable cliché, a horse of a different colour altogether. The snake is an aristocrat in a class society in which status and its symbols are not earned but ascribed. The toad is a commoner whose knowledge and expertise garnered through personal effort count for nothing beside the merit which belongs to the snake by some unspecified right such as birth or wealth. No amount of brightness or ability on the part of the toad is going to alter the position ordained for him. The few but potent words left with him by the snake embody a stern, utilitarian view of education which would tie the acquisition of skills to the availability of scope for their practice.

I have chosen those two little examples from Nigeria's vast and varied treasury of oral literature to show how such stories can combine in a most admirable manner the aesthetic qualities of a successful work of imagination with those homiletic virtues demanded of active definers and custodians of society's values.

But we must not see the role of literature only in terms of providing latent support for things as they are, for it does also offer the kinetic energy necessary for social transition and change. If we tend to dwell more on stability it is only because society itself does aspire to, and indeed requires, longer periods of rest than of turmoil. But literature is also deeply concerned with change. That little fragment about the king who insulted his subjects by breaking their kola-nut in his mouth is a clear incitement to rebellion. But even more illuminating in this connection because of its subtlety is the story of the snake and the toad which at first sight may appear to uphold privilege but at another level of signification does in fact contain the seeds of revolution, the portents of the dissolution of an incompetent oligarchy. The brilliant makers of that story, by denying sympathetic attractiveness to

the snake, are exposing him in the fullness of time to the
harsh tenets of a revolutionary justice.

I think I have now set a wide-ranging enough background
to attempt an answer to the rhetorical question: What has
literature got to do with it?

In the first place, what does "it" stand for? Is it something
concrete like increasing the GNP or something metaphysical
like the *It* which is the object of the quest in Gabriel Okara's
novel *The Voice?*

I should say that my "it" begins with concrete aspirations
like economic growth, health for all, education which actually educates, etc., etc., but soon reveals an umbilical link
with a metaphysical search for abiding values. In other
words, I am saying that development or modernization is not
merely, or even primarily, a question of having lots of money
to spend or blueprints drawn up by the best experts available;
it is in a critical sense a question of the mind and the will.
And I am saying that the mind and the will belong first and
foremost to the domain of stories. In the beginning was the
Word, or the Mind, as an alternative rendering has it. It was
the Word or the Mind that began the story of creation.

So it is with the creation of human societies. And what
Nigeria is aiming to do is nothing less than the creation of a
new place and a new people. And she needs must have the
creative energy of stories to initiate and sustain that work.

Our ancestors created their different polities with myths
embodying their varying perceptions of reality. Every people
everywhere did the same. The Jews had their Old Testament
on account of which early Islam honoured them as the people of the Book. The following passage appears in a brilliant
essay in *Publications of the Modern Language Association of
America:*

The ideals that Homer portrayed in Achilles, Hector and Ulysses played a large role in the formation of the Greek character. Likewise when the Anglo-Saxons huddled around their hearth fires, stories of heroes like Beowulf helped define them as a people, through articulating their values and defining their goals in relation to the cold, alien world around them.[7]

In the essay from which I took that passage the authors set out to demonstrate in detail the potentiality of literature to reform the self in a manner analogous to the processes of psychoanalysis: eliciting deep or unconsciously held primary values and then bringing conscious reflection or competing values to bear on them. The authors underscore the interesting point made by Roy Schafer that psychoanalysis itself is an essay into story-telling. People who go through psychoanalysis tell the analyst about themselves and others in the past and present. In making interpretations the competent analyst reorganizes and retells these stories in such a way that the problematic and incoherent self consciously told at the beginning of the analysis is sorted out to the benefit and sanity of the client.

It would be impossible and indeed inappropriate to pursue this perceptive and tremendously important analogy between literature and psychoanalysis any further here, but I must quote its concluding sentence:

. . . if as Kohut, Meissner and others suggest the self has an inherent teleology for growth and cohesion, then literature can have an important and profound positive effect as well, functioning as a kind of bountiful, nourishing matrix for a healthy, developing psyche.[8]

This is putting into scientific language what our ancestors had known all along and reminds one of the common man who, on being told the meaning of "prose," exclaimed:

"Look at that! So I have been speaking prose all my life without knowing it."

The matter is really quite simple. Literature, whether handed down by word of mouth or in print, gives us a second handle on reality; enabling us to encounter in the safe, manageable dimensions of make-believe the very same threats to integrity that may assail the psyche in real life; and at the same time providing through the self-discovery which it imparts a veritable weapon for coping with these threats whether they are found within problematic and incoherent selves or in the world around us. What better preparation can a people desire as they begin their journey into the strange, revolutionary world of modernization?

Postscript:
James Baldwin
(1924–1987)

SINCE JAMES BALDWIN passed away in his adopted home, France, on the last day of November 1987, the many and varied tributes to him, like the blind men's versions of the elephant, have been consistent in one detail—the immensity, the sheer prodigality of endowment.

When my writing first began to yield small rewards in the way of free travel, UNESCO came along and asked where would I like to go. Without hesitation I said: U.S.A. and Brazil. And so I came to the Americas for the first time in 1963.

An address presented at the Memorial Service for James Baldwin on 16 December 1987, at the University of Massachusetts, Amherst, where he was a member of the faculty and returned to teach at intervals.

My intention, which was somewhat nebulous to begin with, was to find out how the Africans of the diaspora were faring in the two largest countries of the New World. In UNESCO files, however, it was stated with greater precision. I was given a fellowship to enable me to study literary trends and to meet and exchange ideas with writers.

I did indeed make very many useful contacts: John O. Killens, Langston Hughes, Ralph Ellison, Paule Marshall, Leroy Jones and so on; and for good measure, Arthur Miller. They were all wonderful to me. And yet there was no way I could hide from myself or my sponsors my sense of disappointment that one particular meeting could not happen because the man concerned was away in France. And that was the year of *The Fire Next Time!*

Before I came to America I had discovered and read *Go Tell It on the Mountain,* and been instantly captivated. For me it combined the strange and familiar in a way that was entirely new. I went to the United States Information Service Library in Lagos to see what other material there might be *by* or *on* this man. There was absolutely nothing. So I offered a couple of suggestions and such was the persuasiveness of newly independent Africans in those days that when next I looked in at the Library they had not only Baldwin but Richard Wright as well.

I had all my schooling in the educational system of colonial Nigeria. In that system Americans, when they were featured at all, were dismissed summarily by our British administrators as loud and vulgar. Their universities which taught such subjects as dish-washing naturally produced the half-baked noisy political agitators some of whom were now rushing up and down the country because they had acquired no proper skills.

But there was one American book which the colonial educators considered of sufficient value to be exempted from the general censure of things American and actually be prescribed reading in my high school. It was the autobiography of Booker T. Washington: *Up from Slavery.*

This bizarre background probably explains why my first encounter with Baldwin's writing was such a miraculous experience. Nothing that I had heard or read or seen quite prepared me for the Baldwin phenomenon. Needless to say my education was entirely silent about W. E. B. Du Bois who as I later discovered had applied *his* experience of what he called "the strange meaning of being black" in America to ends and insights radically different from Washington's.

A major aspect of my re-education was to see (and what comfort it gave me!) that Baldwin was neither an aberration nor was he likely to be a flash in the pan. He brought a new sharpness of vision, a new energy of passion, a new perfection of language to battle the incubus of race which Dubois had prophesied would possess our century—which prophecy itself had a long pedigree through the slave revolts back into Africa where, believe it or not, a seventeenth-century Igbo priest-king Eze Nri had declared slavery an abomination. I say *believe it or not* because this personage and many others like him in different parts of Africa do not fit the purposes of your history books.

When at last I met Jimmy in person in the jungles of Florida in 1980 I actually greeted him with *Mr. Baldwin, I presume!* You should have seen his eyes dancing, his remarkable face working in ripples of joyfulness. During the four days we spent down there I saw how easy it was to make Jimmy smile; and how the world he was doomed to inhabit would remorselessly deny him that simple benediction.

Baldwin and I were invited by the African Literature Association to open its annual conference in Gainesville with a public conversation. As we stepped into a tremendous ovation in the packed auditorium of the Holiday Inn, Baldwin was in particularly high spirits. I thought the old preacher in him was reacting to the multitude.

He went to the podium and began to make his opening statements. Within minutes a mystery voice came over the public address system and began to hurl racial insults at him and me. I will see that moment to the end of my life. The happiness brutally wiped off Baldwin's face; the genial manner gone; the eyes flashing in defiant combativeness; the voice incredibly calm and measured. And the words of remorseless prophecy began once again to flow.

One of the few hopeful examples of leadership in Africa was terminated abruptly two months ago. Captain Thomas Sankara, leader of Burkina Faso, was murdered in his fourth year of rule by his second-in-command. The world did not pay too much attention to yet another game of musical chairs by power-hungry soldiers in Africa. In any event, Sankara was a brash young man with Marxist leanings who recently had the effrontery to read a lecture to a visiting Head of State who happened to be none other than President Mitterand of France himself. According to press reports of the incident, Mitterand, who is a socialist veteran in his own right, rose to the occasion. He threw away his prepared speech and launched into an hour-long counter-attack in which he must have covered much ground. But perhaps the sting was in the tail: "Sankara is a disturbing person. With him it is impossible to sleep in peace. He does not leave your conscience alone."[1]

I have no doubt that Mitterand meant his comment as

praise for his young and impatient host. But it was also a deadly arraignment and even conviction. Principalities and powers do not tolerate those who interrupt the sleep of their consciences. That Baldwin got away with it for forty years was a miracle. Except of course that he didn't get away; he paid dearly every single day of those years, every single hour of those days.

What was his crime that we should turn him into a man of sadness, this man inhabited by a soul so eager to be loved and to smile? His demands were so few and so simple.

His bafflement, childlike—which does not mean simpleminded but deeply profound and saintly—comes across again and again and nowhere better perhaps than in his essay "Fifth Avenue, Uptown."

> Negroes want to be treated like men: a perfectly straightforward statement containing seven words. People who have mastered Kant, Hegel, Shakespeare, Marx, Freud and the Bible find this statement impenetrable.[2]

This failure to comprehend turns out to be, as one might have suspected, a wilful, obdurate refusal. And for good reason. For let's face it, that sentence, simple and innocent-looking though it may seem, is in reality a mask for a profoundly subversive intent to re-order the world. And the world, viewed from the high point of the pyramid where its controllers reside, is working perfectly well and sitting firm.

Egypt's Pharaoh, according to the myth of the Israelites, faced the same problem when a wild-eyed man walked up to him with a simple demand, four words long: "Let my people go!" We are not told that he rushed off to his office to sign their exit visa. On the contrary.

So neither history nor legend encourages us to believe that

a man who sits on his fellow will some day climb down on the basis of sounds reaching him from below. And yet we must consider how so much more dangerous our already very perilous world would become if the oppressed everywhere should despair altogether of invoking reason and humanity to arbitrate their cause. This is the value and the relevance, into the foreseeable future, of James Baldwin.

As long as injustice exists, whether it be within the American nation itself or between it and its neighbours; as long as a tiny cartel of rich, creditor nations can hold the rest in iron chains of usury; so long as one third or less of mankind eats well and often to excess while two thirds and more live perpetually with hunger; as long as white people who constitute a mere fraction of the human race consider it natural and even righteous to dominate the rainbow majority whenever and wherever they are thrown together; and—the oldest of them all—the discrimination by men against women, as long as it persists; the words of James Baldwin will be there to bear witness and to inspire and elevate the struggle for human freedom.

Notes

1: An Image of Africa: Racism in Conrad's Heart of Darkness *(p. 1)*

1. Albert J. Guerard, introduction to *Heart of Darkness,* New York, New American Library, 1950, p. 9.

2. Joseph Conrad, *Heart of Darkness and The Secret Sharer,* New York, New American Library, 1950, p. 66.

3. F. R. Leavis, *The Great Tradition,* London, Chatto and Windus, 1948; second impression 1950, p. 177.

4. Conrad, *Heart of Darkness,* op. cit., pp. 105–6.

5. Ibid., p. 106.

6. Ibid., p. 78.

7. Ibid., p. 78.

8. Ibid., p. 148.

9. Ibid., p. 153.

10. Ibid., p. 82.

11. Ibid., p. 124.

12. Conrad, quoted in Jonah Raskin, *The Mythology of Imperialism,* New York, Random House, 1971, p. 143.

13. Conrad, *Heart of Darkness,* op. cit., p. 142.

14. Conrad, quoted in Bernard C. Meyer, M.D., *Joseph Conrad: A Psychoanalytic Biography,* Princeton University Press, 1967, p. 30.

15. Ibid., p. 30.

16. Frank Willett, *African Art,* New York, Praeger, 1971, pp. 35–6.

17. About the omission of the Great Wall of China I am indebted to "The Journey of Marco Polo" as re-created by artist Michael-Foreman, published by *Pegasus* magazine, New York, 1974.

18. *Christian Science Monitor,* Boston, 25 November 1974, p. 11.

2: *Impediments to Dialogue Between North and South (p. 21)*

1. Janheinz Jahn, *Muntu,* New York, Grove Press, 1979, 14th edn., p. 20.
2. *New York Times Book Review,* 13 May 1979.

4: *The Novelist as Teacher (p. 40)*

1. W. H. Whiteley (ed.), *A Selection of African Prose,* Oxford, Clarendon Press, 1964.

5: *The Writer and His Community (p. 47)*

1. Herbert M. Cole, *Mbari: Art and Life Among the Owerri Igbo,* Bloomington, Indiana University Press, 1982, p. 100.
2. C. H. Kane, *Ambiguous Adventure,* 1962, René Juillard, trans. from the French by Katherine Woods, New York, Collier, 1963, pp. 105–6.
3. Stanley Diamond, *In Search of the Primitive,* New Brunswick, N. J., Transaction Books, 1974.
4. O. Manoni, *Prospero and Caliban,* New York, Praeger, 1966, p. 141.
5. *New York Times Book Review,* 24 October 1982.
6. Anthony Burgess, *Ninety-nine Novels,* London, Alison and Busby, 1984, p. 18.
7. Ibid.
8. Simon Ottenberg, *Masked Rituals of Afikpo,* Seattle and London, University of Washington Press, 1975, p. 74.
9. Chinweizu, *The West and the Rest of Us,* New York, Random House, 1975.
10. J. B. Priestley, *Literature and Western Man,* New York, Harper and Row, 1960, p. 83.

7: *Colonialist Criticism (p. 68)*

1. Iris Andreski, *Old Wives' Tales,* New York, Schocken Books, 1971, p. 26.
2. Charles Larson, *Books Abroad,* Norman, Oklahoma, Winter 1974, p. 69.
3. Chinua Achebe, "Where Angels Fear to Tread," *Nigeria Magazine,* no. 75, Lagos, 1962.
4. Charles Larson, *The Emergence of African Fiction,* Indianapolis, Indiana University Press, 1971, p. 230.
5. Philip Allen, "*Bound to Violence* by Yambo Ouloguem," *Pan-African Journal,* vol. iv, no. 4, New York, Pan-African Institute Inc., Fall 1971, pp. 518–523.
6. Margaret Lawrence, *Long Drums and Cannons,* London, Macmillan, 1968, p. 9.

7. Ivan Van Sertima, *Caribbean Writers*, London, New Beacon, 1968, fore-word.

8. Ibid., p. xiv.

9. Sunday O. Anozie, *Christopher Okigbo*, London, Evans Bros., 1972, p. 17.

10. Adrian A. Roscoe, *Mother Is Gold*, Cambridge University Press, 1971, pp. 98–9.

11. Amos Tutuola, *The Palm-Wine Drinkard*, London, Faber, 1952, p. 100.

12. Ibid., p. 92.

13. Camara Laye, interviewed by J. Steven Rubin, *Africa Report*, Washington, D.C., May 1972, p. 22.

14. Davidson Abioseh Nicol, *The Truly Married Woman and Other Stories*, London, Fontana, 1965, introduction.

15. Kofi Awoonor, quoted in Per Wästberg (ed.), *The Writer in Modern Africa*, Uppsala, Almqvist & Wiksell.

16. Frank Willett, *African Art*, New York, Praeger, 1971, p. 102.

8: *Thoughts on the African Novel (p. 91)*

1. Chinua Achebe, *Arrow of God*, London, William Heinemann, 1964, p. 112.

2. Eldred Jones, "The Essential Soyinka," *Introduction to Nigerian Literature*, Bruce King (ed.), Lagos, University of Lagos; London, Evans, 1971, p. 132.

3. Ibid., p. 121.

9: *Work and Play in Tutuola's* The Palm-Wine Drinkard *(p. 100)*

1. Adrian A. Roscoe, *Mother Is Gold*, Cambridge University Press, 1971, pp. 98–99.

2. Amos Tutuola, *The Palm-Wine Drinkard*, London, Faber, 1952, p. 7.

3. Ibid., p. 7.

4. Ibid., p. 39.

5. Ibid., p. 84.

6. Ibid., p. 85.

7. Ibid., p. 69.

8. Ibid., p. 71.

9. Ibid.

10. Ibid.

11. Ibid.

12: *Language and the Destiny of Man (p. 127)*

1. Sonia Cole, *The Prehistory of East Africa*, New York, Macmillan, 1963, pp. 122–3.

2. G. E. Igwe and M. M. Green, *Igbo Language Course,* Ibadan, Oxford University Press (Nigeria), 1967.

3. Mugo Gatheru, *A Child of Two Worlds,* London, Heinemann Educational Books, 1966, p. 40.

4. Ulli Beier (ed.), *The Origin of Life and Death,* London, Heinemann Educational Books, 1966.

5. Camara Laye, *The African Child,* London, Fontana, 1959, p. 53.

6. Jerome Rothenberg (ed.), *Shaking the Pumpkin,* Garden City, N.Y., Doubleday, 1972, p. 45.

7. T. S. Eliot, Four Quartets, *"East Coker,"* New York, Harcourt Brace Jovanovich, Inc.

8. T. S. Eliot, "Little Gidding," Ibid.

9. George Orwell, "Politics and the English Language," in *Essays,* Garden City, N.Y., Doubleday, 1954.

10. Dr. F. Nwako, "Disorders in Medical Education," *Nsukkascope,* Nsukka, 1972.

11. Beier, op. cit.

12. Edmund Leach, *Lévi-Strauss,* London, Fontana/Collins, 1970.

13. Beier, op. cit.

13: The Truth of Fiction (p. 139)

1. Matthew Arnold, "Memorial Verses," *The Works of Matthew Arnold,* vol. 1, New York, AMS Press, 1970, p. 251.

2. Frank Kermode, *The Sense of an Ending,* New York, Oxford University Press, 1967.

3. Ibid.

14: What Has Literature Got to Do with It? (p. 155)

1. *Proceedings of the Tokyo Colloquium,* October 1981.

2. W. Arthur Lewis, "The State of Development Theory," *American Economic Review,* 1984; reprinted in *Economic Impact,* 49, 1985, p. 82.

3. J. K. Galbraith, in *Proceedings: American Academy and Institute of Arts and Letters,* second series, no. 35, New York, 1984.

4. Proceedings of the Tokyo Colloquium, published in *The Daily Yomuiri,* 18 November 1981.

5. The Vice-Chancellor of Ibadan University, Professor Ayo Banjo, was reported as making the point that Ibadan does not teach mass communications and yet "has produced most of the best writers in Nigerian journalism today": *Sunday Concord,* 16 February 1986.

6. Ulli Beier (ed.), *The Origin of Life and Death,* London, Heinemann Educational Books, 1966.

7. M. W. Alcorn and M. Bracher, "Literature, Psychoanalysis and the Reformation of the Self. A New Direction for Reader-Response Theory," *Publications of the Modern Language Association of America,* New York, May 1985, p. 350.

8. Ibid., p. 352.

Postscript (p. 172)

1. *New York Times,* 23 August 1987, p. 10.

2. James Baldwin, "Fifth Avenue, Uptown," first published in *Esquire,* June 1960. Reprinted in *The Price of the Ticket,* New York, St. Martin's/Marek, 1985, p. 211.

Index

Chinua Achebe was born in Nigeria in 1930. He was raised in the large village of Ogidi, one of the first centers of Anglican missionary work in Eastern Nigeria, and is a graduate of University College, Ibadan.

His early career in radio ended abruptly in 1966, when he left his post as Director of External Broadcasting in Nigeria during the national upheaval that led to the Biafran War. Mr. Achebe joined the Biafran Ministry of Information and represented Biafra on various diplomatic and fund-raising missions. He was appointed Senior Research Fellow at the University of Nigeria, Nsukka, and began lecturing widely abroad.

From 1972 to 1976, and again in 1987 to 1988, Mr. Achebe was a Professor of English at the University of Massachusetts, Amherst, and also for one year at the University of Connecticut, Storrs.

Characterized by the *New York Times Magazine* as "one of Nigeria's most gifted writers," Chinua Achebe has published novels, short stories, essays, and children's books. His volume of poetry, *Christmas in Biafra,* written during the Biafran War, was the joint winner of the first Commonwealth Poetry Prize. Of his novels, *Arrow of God* is winner of the New Statesman–Jock Campbell Award, and *Anthills of the Savannah* was a finalist for the 1987 Booker Prize in England.

Mr. Achebe has received numerous honors from around the world, including the Honorary Fellowship of the American Academy and Institute of Arts and Letters, as well as twelve honorary doctorates from universities in England, Scotland, the United States, Canada, and Nigeria. He is also the recipient of

Nigeria's highest award for intellectual achievement, the Nigerian National Merit Award.

Mr. Achebe lives with his wife in Nigeria. They have four children.